THE VIA CRUCIS

Anna—
You are truly God's
masterpiece, created in Chirst
Jesus for great adventures prepared
for you before the creation of
the world — Eph 2:10 - May
you understand He loves you
always — Daddy's is not
mad! May you always
seek His heart!
Shawn

THE VIA CRUCIS

Shawn Small

Providence House Publishers
WWW.PROVIDENCEHOUSE.COM
FRANKLIN, TENNESSEE

Printed in the United States of America

12   11   10   09   08   1   2   3   4   5

Library of Congress Control Number: 2007942136

ISBN: 978-1-57736-401-6

Cover and illustrations by Jenny Slaver
Cover and page design by LeAnna Massingille

PROVIDENCE HOUSE PUBLISHERS
238 Seaboard Lane • Franklin, Tennessee 37067
www.providencehouse.com
800-321-5692

For

Allen Groff
who, in the twilight of his life,
continues his journey of faith
full of passion, joy, and a bit of mischief.

Keith Wheeler
who exemplifies what it
means to carry the cross.

Grandma Marie Lindgren
who taught me to read and
said, "You ought to write a book."

And to all the devoted church fathers in
history who paved stones on the
path toward the via crucis.

Contents

contents

Foreword

In 1985, I felt that God was inviting me to begin a unique pilgrimage. I built a large, wooden cross and began walking with it to share His love with people along the roadsides and marketplaces of this world. More than twenty years later, I continue to carry this cross.

By the grace of God, I have carried it thousands of miles, through a multitude of nations on all seven continents. I have carried the cross into regions at war and peace. The cross has visited the warm islands of the South Pacific and the bitter cold of the Antarctic. I have taken it from the heights of the Himalayas to the depths of the Jordan Valley. I have walked with the cross through jungles of Africa and South America, and across the deserts of the Middle East. I am not an adventurer or world traveler. I am a pilgrim follower of Jesus trying not just to carry a cross, but also to live in the way of the cross.

I don't completely understand how carrying a piece of wood on my shoulder can be very effective in God's great plan, but I do believe that God uses it to draw people so I can share His message of love and salvation. The cross is heavy. I get dirty, tired, hungry, and thirsty. I get blisters and sunburn. Often, people don't understand. Sometimes people laugh. It can be a very lonely and humbling experience. Maybe that is the point. I have found that when my pride, comfort, and security are taken away, I have to lean on something besides myself. There has to be a laying down of our rights and reputation—a crucifixion before there is a resurrection. It is in dying that we live.

On my journey, I have had the privilege of meeting some of the most incredible people you could imagine. Shawn Small is one of those people. He joined me in the fall of 2000 to carry the cross in Madagascar and some of the neighboring island nations just of the eastern coast of Africa. As I walked African roadsides with Shawn, I came to know a man who had allowed God to shape his life by the cross.

In a small village in the Islamic Republic of the Comoros, we had finished for the day and were preparing to leave. As usual, we were surrounded by a crowd of curious onlookers, eager and full of questions. Suddenly, people began to laugh and point. On the other side of the road emerged a dirty, disheveled young man. Some called him demon-possessed, others called him the village idiot. Either way, he looked wild. He was dirty, smelly, unwanted, and unloved—but not to Shawn. He smiled and tried to communicate with this young man. Suddenly the young man pointed to his shoes. The young man's footwear were soles with the toe portion cut out for feet that had long ago outgrown the shoes. Like the young man, they were dirty, smelly, and torn. Shawn's shoes were new, whole, and (relatively speaking) expensive. Without hesitation, Shawn smiled, took off his shoes, and gave them to the young man, who smiled and promptly gave his old shoes in return.

What happened next was truly beautiful. Shawn squeezed his feet into the old, stinky shoes and smiled. He valued the young man enough to give his nice, comfortable shoes to the one others called an idiot and a demon. He honored the man by receiving his poor, smelly gift. In return, he gave him dignity. Weeks later, Shawn developed a rash on his feet where the shoes had been. To this day, he bears scars on his feet from wearing those shoes.

It reminds you a little of Jesus, doesn't it? At the cross, Jesus gave what was costly. At the cross, we give up what is old, torn, and smelly. We walk away with new life, and Jesus bears the scars. When we take up our cross, we will be marked as we walk in the Via Crucis.

Jesus called His followers to travel the roads of life as pilgrims. I invite you as a pilgrim to join Shawn in this book as we follow Jesus together in a pure and simple way along the Via Crucis. Come walk in the shoes of a pilgrim, but be warned . . . it will probably leave you marked for life!!

Keith Wheeler
A pilgrim follower of Jesus
www.kw.org

Preface

preface

I have had the unique opportunity to speak across the world in churches of various traditions. Whenever I mention the stations of the cross, I receive a variety of responses. The Protestant response is usually, "Isn't that one of those Catholic practices that they believe earns them a special place in heaven?" My Eastern Orthodox friends say, "That's Western. We are Eastern. It doesn't apply to us." My Catholic brethren usually smile and nod with a look of subtle concurrence, while my nondenominational friends cock their heads like confused puppies. The stations of the cross is one of the most common but misunderstood worship practices in the church today.

The stations of the cross, or via crucis, has always intrigued me. I first became aware of the stations during frequent visits to Ireland in the mid-1990s. Every lovely church that I entered had fourteen artistic renditions of Christ's passion purposefully placed around the sanctuary. These representations were often carved in stone or wood, shaped in stained glass, or created through strikingly painted images.

Though depicted in a multitude of skillful interpretations, the message was always consistent: a determined Christ, with keen eyes set like flint toward Golgotha. His face always depicted the honorable agony of One who had clearly resolved to finish the course set in front of Him, no matter the cost or anguish. Beginning at His condemnation before Pilate, and ending at the entombing of His body, for hundreds of years these stations have inspired the faithful to carry the cross and follow Christ.

After a bit of research, I began to incorporate the stations of the cross into my times of meditation. They were ingrained into my prayer life, and eventually into my psyche. As I have led groups on pilgrimage around the world, I often walk them through the via crucis in remembrance of Christ's sacrifice. The response has always been one of awe and inspired decision.

This book was born out of my passion for the via crucis (the way of the cross). I pray this journey to the cross inspires the reader into greater contemplation of our Lord's sacrifice, and to a practical response to that gift.

How to Use This Book

"If anyone desires to follow after Me he must first take up his cross then follow after Me" (Mark 8:34, author's paraphrase). These loaded words from the Savior have always shaken me to the core. But this statement also begs a question: What, exactly, does it mean to take up our cross? There is no greater nor concise answer to that query than to follow the footsteps of Jesus as He carried the cross toward Golgotha.

Initially, *The Via Crucis* was written as a Lenten devotional for personal meditation during the weeks leading to Easter. Starting on Ash Wednesday, a devotional was written for every day except Sundays. Of course, these devotionals can be read at any time, for the cross is a daily call and challenge that has no single season.

My favorite way to use this devotional is in a community setting. The via crucis translates beautifully into an evening celebration any time of the year, and during almost any occasion. If you are interested in presenting the via crucis in a community setting, refer to appendix A for some ideas.

In this book, each via crucis devotional is written in four distinctive sections. The first page contains art illustrating the daily reading. I would suggest you take a moment to contemplate the image before moving to the Scriptures. Holy Scripture is clearly indicated and written in a chronological order to keep a flow to the story. The next section is the daily reading. These readings are offered from the perspective of a character affected by the story. They may be full of faith, wonder, or even antagonism, depending upon the narrator of the tale. To bring it all together, each section ends with a prayer designed to clarify what it means to carry the cross and follow Christ. When you have finished, I suggest you return to the daily image and take a concluding moment of contemplation.

My prayer is that you experience the presence of Christ through this tiny book. To experience the Transcendent One is to be never content with the world that is. May this book help you to clutch the cross and let loose of the way of self.

Introduction

The via crucis (way of the cross) has been identified for hundreds of years with religious celebrations leading up to Christendom's most holy day of Easter. More commonly known as the stations of the cross, this Catholic practice did not become a standard practice of devotion until the end of the seventeenth century. Yet, this pilgrimage in miniature has deep roots into the life of the body of Christ from the very threshold of its existence.

The way of Christ's suffering, from the Garden of Gethsemane to the rocky hill of Golgotha, was carefully marked out by pious believers from the earliest days. With the conversion of Constantine and his subsequent construction of the Church of the Holy Sepulchre came a frenzy of devoted pilgrims visiting the land of Jesus. Saint Jerome, living in Bethlehem the latter part of his life, testified that crowds of Christians from around the world often came to visit Jerusalem to follow the holy path of their Lord. Still, there is no direct evidence that a set pattern of devotion or liturgy existed at that point.

The financial realities of the common man, however, do not allow for months of leisurely travel for devotion, no matter the depth of religious fervor. So, from the earliest of times, the desire to replicate holy places for those hindered from long pilgrimage was set in the heart of the devout.

In the fifth century, the enthusiastic Bishop of Bologna, Saint Petronious, constructed a few connected chapels to represent the holiest shrines of Jerusalem. This action was possibly inspired by his childhood visit to the holy places in Jerusalem. These memorials at San Stefano, Italy, attracted visitors who referred to the monastery as "Hierusalem." This was the first recorded structure that appears to be the seed for the modern stations, but it was nowhere near what we have today.

Between the twelfth and fourteenth centuries, pilgrims visiting the Holy Land often felt inspired to walk the via sacra (sacred way), a settled route positioned by the Franciscans that followed the footsteps of Christ to Calvary.

The monks set up stopping points along the way, allowing the faithful to contemplate, seek indulgences, and speak heartfelt petitions.

In 1458, English pilgrim William Wey wrote an instructional book for pilgrims visiting the Holy Land for the first time. In this small book, *Itinerary for Pilgrimage to Jerusalem*, the term "stations" was first used to describe these reverential halting places. Surprisingly, the path began at Calvary and ended at Pilate's home. This was reversed in the sixteenth century to the obviously more logical course.

Because of the difficulty of long-distance travel and Moslem Turk control of the Holy Land, numerous reproductions of the Jerusalem holy places were constructed throughout Europe during the fifteenth and sixteenth centuries. The Blessed Alvarez's Dominican chapels in Cordova contained the first recorded paintings of primary scenes from Christ's passion. Many of these reproductions (which seemed to multiply in Renaissance zeal) were marked out in the same number of paces as their counterparts in Jerusalem. Thus, the pious visitor to this replica was able to cover the same distance that a pilgrim walked in the streets of the Holy City of David.

The number of stations has varied over the years, ranging anywhere from seven to thirty-seven. So how did we end up with the sanctioned fourteen stations? Interestingly, Wey's book stated there were fourteen stations, but only five of them match up to the current stations. In 1584, Adrichomious gave us the first twelve stations that correspond exactly to the modern stations in his widely published, church-authorized book entitled *Jerusalem sicut Christi Tempore flourit*. Yet, by the end of the sixteenth century, there was still no unanimous devotion.

It can be said with strong conviction that the current practice of the stations of the cross was developed out of the European reproductions and devotional manuals rather than the actual route in Jerusalem. By the end of the eighteenth century, the arrangement of the stations in church sanctuaries had become common. The Franciscans had realized that most pilgrims would never make it to Jerusalem within their lifetimes, thus they were limited in attaining the indulgences common to the holy sites in Israel. To respond to this dilemma, they suggested erecting coordinating stations in Franciscan churches. In 1686, Pope Innocent IX, realizing few people could travel to the Holy Land because of Moslem political control, granted the petitions of the Franciscans. Faithful parishioners now had the ability to gain indulgences by walking through the stations in their home parishes.

By 1731, Pope Clement XII set the number of stations at fourteen. (Because of the intrinsic relationship between the passion and death of Christ with His resurrection, many modern devotionals on the stations add a fifteenth, resurrection.)

In 1742, Pope Benedict XIV called for the universal church to enrich her sanctuaries "with so great a treasure." Benedict's words were taken to heart by the Western church.

By 1857, the last restriction was removed. The stations were taken out of the hands of the Franciscans and placed into the hands of the bishops, allowing stations to be erected anywhere within a bishop's jurisdiction. Throughout the eighteenth century, the Franciscans passionately preached on the virtues of the stations, and the use of the stations spread rapidly throughout the Roman Catholic world. By the nineteenth century, the practice had become a staple in Catholic prayer books and churches throughout Europe and North America.

This beautiful devotional practice, reflecting the passion of Jesus in our daily lives, echoes the words of our Lord in St. Matthew 16:24, "If anyone desires to be my disciple, you must put aside selfish desire, shoulder your cross, and follow me" (author's paraphrase). The ancient prayer practice of the via crucis captures a renewed sense of accountability for today's Christians. Through the passion of the death of Jesus, we are able to reflect upon the meaning of sacrifice and the price of eternal life.

THE VIA CRUCIS

Anyone who does not take his **cross** and follow me is not worthy of me.

Matthew 10:38

Questions

There is no tale ever told that men would rather find was true.
J. R. R. Tolkien, writing on the Incarnation

He called the people and his disciples to him and said, "If anyone wants to be a follower of mine, let him renounce himself and take up his cross and follow me. Anyone who wants to save his life will lose it; but anyone who loses his life for my sake, and for the sake of the gospel, will save it."
Mark 8:34–35 (NJB)

He said, "The Son of man is destined to suffer grievously, to be rejected by the elders and chief priests and scribes and to be put to death, and to be raised up on the third day." Then, speaking to all, he said, "If anyone wants to be a follower of mine, let him renounce himself and take up his cross every day and follow me."
Luke 9:22–23 (NJB)

Jesus replied to them, "Now the hour has come for the Son of man to be glorified. In all truth I tell you, unless a wheat grain falls into the earth and dies, it remains only a single grain; but if it dies it yields a rich harvest. Anyone who loves his life loses it; anyone who hates his life in this world will keep it for eternal life. Whoever serves me, must follow me, and my servant will be with me wherever I am."
John 12:23–26 (NJB)

Two nights have passed and they still remain in hiding. The Eleven sit in a room darkened not only by the lack of light, but by the loss of their Rabbi's once-constant company. His presence has been replaced with an all-enveloping depression. They had devoted their entire existence to following Him, and now all that remains is a sentiment of abandonment. Had they abandoned Him or had He abandoned them? His body was not the only thing entombed. Their hopes, desires, and lives had died and were buried alongside Him.

His words hung like wraiths haunting all of their thoughts. They had nothing else to do but ponder the last tragic hours of His all-too-short life. The mysterious words that He spoke to them of His imminent end were now blatant. He had said He would suffer a heinous death; He named His accusers days before the events would transpire.

But it was His words about a cross that seemed to trouble them the most. He proclaimed, on more than one occasion, that the cost of following Him was their willingness to carry a cross every day. In fact, He said that they had to lose their lives for the gospel in order to gain life in God. But where was that good news now?

His statements about the cross had caused all of them to be dreadfully uncomfortable. In their minds, thieves, murderers, and the godless were the only ones destined for that specific means of Roman torture. Why would He compare following after Him to the most brutal death sentence their oppressors employed? Yet they now realized that their beloved Master and steadfast friend, the one they all believed to be Messiah, had carried a criminal's weight.

His words about carrying a cross, once uncomfortable, now tormented this group of men who were gradually pining away in the darkness. They wonder what their lives were worth. What was His life worth? So here they cower as the last few hours of their beloved Jesus' life replay in their minds over and over again.

This way of the cross began late in the evening just two nights ago in a garden called Gethsemane.

Lord Jesus Christ, have mercy upon me.

This day, I begin a journey.
I am not sure where this expedition of the heart will lead me,
yet I am assured that You will guide my steps.
Help me, through the story of Your passion,
to discover what it means to take up the cross
and follow in Your footsteps.

The Word of God declares,
unless a wheat grain falls into the earth and dies,
it remains only a single grain;
but if it dies, it yields a rich harvest.
Help me to die to self and find life in You.
Anyone who loves his life will lose it;
anyone who hates his life in this world
will keep it for eternity.

Help me break away from the appeal of the world
and draw toward the eternal.
Whoever serves You must follow You,
and Your servant will be with You wherever You are.
Help me to serve You and follow You anywhere.

Help me journey from Gethsemane to the empty tomb,
discovering what it means to carry the cross and follow You.

Lord Jesus Christ, have mercy upon me.

Sacrifice gives you **no pleasure,**
burnt offering **you do not** desire.
Sacrifice to **GOD**
is a **broken** spirit,
a broken [crushed] **heart**
you never scorn.

Psalm 51:16-17 (NJB)

Gethsemane

There are only two kinds of people in the end: those who say to God, "Thy will be done," and those to whom God says in the end, "Thy will be done."

C. S. Lewis, *The Great Divorce*

Then Jesus came with them to a plot of land called Gethsemane; and he said to his disciples, "Stay here while I go over there to pray." He took Peter and the two sons of Zebedee with him. And he began to feel sadness and anguish. Then he said to them, "My soul is sorrowful to the point of death. Wait here and stay awake with me." And going on a little further he fell on his face and prayed. "My Father," he said, "if it is possible, let this cup pass me by. Nevertheless, let it be as you, not I, would have it." He came back to the disciples and found them sleeping, and he said to Peter, "So you had not the strength to stay awake with me for one hour? Stay awake, and pray not to be put to the test. The spirit is willing enough, but human nature is weak." Again, a second time, he went away and prayed: "My Father," he said, "if this cup cannot pass by, but I must drink it, your will be done!" And he came back again and found them sleeping, their eyes were so heavy. Leaving them there, he went away again and prayed for a third time, repeating the same words.

Matthew 26:36–44 (NJB)

The Passover supper had revealed infinitely more than His few followers understood. "Take and eat this bread for this is my body, broken for you. Drink from this cup, for it is my blood, poured out for the forgiveness of sins." Jesus knew the seeds of Eucharist were planted in unknowing hearts. In a few days, clarity would illuminate their spirits with a glory hidden from the dawn of creation; but tonight all seemed so shadowed and frightening.

Seeking a fragment of solace in His final few moments before the vast torrent of hate overtook Him, Jesus walked with His Eleven to Gethsemane. Oh, how He loved the peace and solitude of this place! Whenever He visited Jerusalem, He set time aside to seek the Father in this ancient olive grove.

But tonight was different. He did not come seeking peace or solitude. He arrived with an earnest request. Gathering His three closest companions, Jesus pleaded with them to pray as He went before the Father. As He moved a mere stone's throw away, terror and anguish overwhelmed Him.

Heavenly creatures had gathered from the ends of creation to witness this battle which had commenced in the most unlikely of arenas. The Prophet that challenged Pharisee and demon alike threw Himself to the ground and prayed, "Abba, Father! I beg you, take this cup away from me." The next moment of silence froze the invisible spectators.

"But let it be as You, not I, would have it." With those words, Abba released one of the angelic beings to emerge from its otherworldly cover, bringing the Son an offering of strength—the strength necessary to fulfill God's will.

Discovering His three friends in oblivious slumber, Jesus knew this would be His battle alone. How ironic that this garden was named the Place of Crushing; like olives in the press, He would be crushed.

In climactic agony, blood trickled from His brow in great drops. His will was sacrificed as this simple carpenter from Nazareth declared, "Not my will but Thy will be done!" The fountain that would soon flood the streets of Jerusalem began to flow in this tiny garden known as Gethsemane.

Lord Jesus Christ, have mercy upon me.

As You entered Gethsemane on the fateful night of Your
betrayal, You came frightened and sorrowful.
Although You arrived with eleven companions,
loneliness was to be your only attendant. Knowing what You
would soon face, You asked the Father one request:
"Abba, Father! I beg you, take this cup away from me."
But there was no other way.
This was the road set from the very foundations of creation.
So, with all your strength, you proclaimed,
"Not my will but Thy will be done!"
You would allow Yourself to be crushed by the Father.
That crushing would release oil that would heal our souls
and a new wine that would bring about
the redemption of mankind.

God, I struggle with my Gethsemane moments.
Often I feel frightened, sorrowful, and alone.
I find myself crying out for Your will in my life.
Yet when I am presented with that will,
I do not have the courage to be obedient.
I often beg You to take this cup away, yet it remains.
Give me the strength to follow the leading of Christ
and proclaim, "Not my will but Thy will be done in my life."
Father, You do not ask me for a sacrifice or I would give it.
You desire me to have a broken and crushed heart.
This moment I ask You to give me the strength
to release my heart into Your hands. May my life be
overtaken by Your presence. Allow the Holy Spirit to use me
as a vessel of healing and redemption. May I always allow
the decisions of my heart to be a reflection of Gethsemane.

Lord Jesus Christ, have mercy upon me.

Even my trusted **friend**
on whom I relied,
who **shared** my table,
takes **advantage** of me.

Psalm 41:9 (NJB)

Betrayed

Cowards die many times before their deaths;
The valiant never taste of death but once.
William Shakespeare, *Julius Caesar*

Then one of the Twelve, the man called Judas Iscariot, went to the chief priests and said, "What are you prepared to give me if I hand him over to you?" They paid him thirty silver pieces, and from then onwards he began to look for an opportunity to betray him.
Matthew 26:14–16 (NJB)

"In truth I tell you, one of you is about to betray me. The Son of man is going to his fate, as the scriptures say he will, but alas for that man by whom the Son of man is betrayed! Better for that man if he had never been born!"
Matthew 26:21, 24 (NJB)

"Look, the hour has come when the Son of man is to be betrayed into the hands of sinners." And suddenly while he was still speaking, Judas, one of the Twelve, appeared, and with him a large number of men armed with swords and clubs, sent by the chief priests and elders of the people. Now the traitor had arranged a sign with them saying, "The one I kiss, he is the man. Arrest him." So he went up to Jesus at once and said, "Greetings, Rabbi," and kissed him. Jesus said, "Judas, are you betraying the Son of man with a kiss?"
Matthew 26:45, 47–49 and Luke 22:48 (NJB)

Only a few hours ago this place was an ordinary farmer's field just outside the gates of Jerusalem. Tonight changed that fact; this pasture is now infamous. Its new name: the Field of Blood. From this point forward, a one-time grazing field will become a graveyard for foreigners and unknown vagrants who die in the city and are not worthy of a proper burial. All of this because of the silhouetted figure hanging from a lone tree that stands in the middle of this tiny plot.

Some would say he was the most promising of the Twelve. Unlike the rough and tumble Galilean fisherman, or the other disciples with shaded pasts, this one was properly educated and of the most excellent pedigree. In fact, he was the only Judean of the lot. But could what they say be true? Was he a traitor? Did he turn against the very One he followed for three years?

What was his motivation? Maybe he began to think that Jesus of Nazareth was a false Messiah. Was he outraged with Jesus' seeming indifference to the law or His association with shady characters? Maybe he assumed that this action would force the Chosen One into asserting His messianic powers. We will never know for sure.

What we do know is that he sought out the enemies of His Master just days before to ask what price they were willing to pay for betrayal. And what was his fee? This man of great promise sold the life of his Rabbi for thirty pieces of silver.

When the schemer's plan took place, it caught almost everyone off guard. In the middle of the night, in a secluded garden, the soldiers and guards arrived as an angry mob. The betrayer walked through the crowd.

Jesus turned to him and spoke saying, "Good friend, do what you have come to do." With that, Judas greeted his Rabbi with a kiss on the cheek. "Judas, are you betraying the Son of man with a kiss?"

The words of accusation and those eyes of love pierced the man's soul. Suddenly, the thirty pieces of silver Judas carried hidden in his tunic felt like a millstone hung around his neck. What had he done? He had betrayed an innocent man. He had betrayed his friend.

Rushing to the temple, Judas rid himself of the blood money. Assuming forgiveness was no longer an option, he could not bear the weight of his guilt. So in this field, he ended his life. That silhouetted body hanging against a gray morning sky bitterly proclaimed to the ages, "I, Judas, betrayed my Lord!"

Lord Jesus Christ, have mercy upon me.

Father, this one that betrayed You had followed You for three years. He earnestly listened to Your teachings. He saw You heal the sick and free the oppressed. You warmly patted his back as a steadfast friend. He laughed and wept with You, the Messiah. He beheld You walking in an authority he thought impossible.

Yet, this man, Judas Iscariot, betrayed his Master for the redemption price of a slave. He allowed Satan to consume his thoughts and influence his decisions. In the end, turning to Your enemies brought him utter hopelessness and despair. The price of betrayal became the bane of his soul. Alone, desperate, and marked, he took the coward's course and ended his life.

As much as it pains me, Lord, I must admit that there are times I have betrayed you. Even though I have witnessed Your presence in my life, I have often sold my soul for the price of sin. Father, redeem me from the works of Satan. Please forgive any obstinate transgression in my heart. Help me to turn away from the sin that so easily distracts me from Your truth and will for my life. I never want to be Your enemy. I do not want to be branded as a betrayer. I want to be known as a faithful servant and friend. Permit me to always recognize forgiveness and allow me to have the courage to possess a clean heart. Remind me that I am never forsaken in Your presence.

Lord Jesus Christ, have mercy upon me.

By
oppression
and
judgment
he was taken away.

Isaiah 53:8 (RSV)

Arrested

Death comes nearer, our enemy encircles us, and the circle grows narrower. Let us die like Christians.
author unknown

So Judas brought the cohort to this place together with guards sent by the chief priests and the Pharisees, all with lanterns and torches and weapons. . . . Jesus came forward and said, "Who are you looking for?" They answered, "Jesus the Nazarene." He said, "I am he." . . . When Jesus said to them, "I am he," they moved back and fell on the ground. . . . "If I am the one you are looking for, let these others go." . . . Simon Peter, who had a sword, drew it and struck the high priest's servant, cutting off his right ear. The servant's name was Malchus. Jesus said to Peter, "Put your sword back in its scabbard; am I not to drink the cup that the Father has given me?" Touching the man's ear [Jesus] healed him. Then all the disciples deserted him and ran away. Then Jesus said to the chief priests and captains of the Temple guard and elders who had come for him, "Am I [leading a rebellion], that you had set out with swords and clubs? When I was among you in the Temple day after day you never made a move to lay hands on me. But this is your hour; this is the reign of darkness."
John 18:3–11; Matthew 26:47–56; and Luke 22:51–53 (NJB)

I came to this garden tonight clearly knowing friend from enemy. I had a righteous duty to fulfill, but the blood that covers my hands and robe leaves me staggered. How could I have been so mistaken? How was I so blind and deaf to the truth? I was to represent the chief priest in this matter of national security. I approached this garden of shadows in the early morning with a warrant for the arrest of a dangerous insurrectionist. At least, I was assuming he was a great threat, by the amount of armed temple guards and soldiers that accompanied us.

We had not seized him in the temple because of his enormous influence with the common people. There was even talk amongst them that he was the Messiah returned. That sort of talk even upsets the Romans. We thought him a false Messiah. Certainly, the priests and leaders of the people did not acknowledge him as a prophet. But what did he do that was so heinous that it called for a cowardly seizure in the middle of the night?

When we arrived and the traitor gave the sign, this Nazarene asked for whom we were looking. When we spoke his name, he replied with "I am he." The entire mob drew back in terror, and many fell to the ground. I covered my ears (how ironic) because of the utter majesty of his words.

Composing ourselves once more, but not nearly as confidently, we again approached. That is when one of his zealous followers made a desperate attempt to cut off my head. I ducked his awkward sword thrust, which saved my neck, but still sent a biting pain to the right side of my head. Down on the ground, in plain sight, was my bloodied ear. Instinctively, I grabbed my head. Blood sprayed over me and covered my hands.

I can only relay portions of the words of this Jesus that followed. " . . . die by the sword . . . twelve legions of angels . . . drink the cup the Father. . . ." The next thing I experienced was his hand on my head and the pain instantly ceasing. My ear was wholly restored. Was it not for the blood that covered me, I would not have believed that I had been wounded.

All his followers fled in great haste, leaving him alone. He lovingly looked into my eyes, then spoke to the startled mob saying, "This is your hour; this is the reign of darkness."

I came to this garden tonight clearly knowing friend from enemy. How could I have been so mistaken?

Lord Jesus Christ, have mercy upon me.

They came to the garden veiled in darkness;
Allow me to shine forth in darkness.

They refused to acknowledge You as Messiah
and it drove their hatred;
I acknowledge You as Messiah.
May it compel me in steadfast love.

They sought You, Lord, for harm;
Let me seek You for healing.

When You spoke, "I am," they stumbled back in terror;
When You speak, "I am," may I bow in worship.

One of Yours tried to defend with the sword.
May I find my defense in Your presence alone.

Those that proclaimed themselves
Your followers fled in the night.
Help me to never flee from Your presence,
but remain close to Your heart.

You drank of the cup of the Father's will.
Give me the strength to also drink of the cup of His will.

Lord Jesus Christ, have mercy upon me.

I heard your **voice**
in the **garden**
and I was full of
fear and **dread**
because I was naked,
so I hid.

Genesis 3:10
(author's paraphrase)

Naked

The tears which I had been holding back streamed down, and I let them flow as freely as they would, making of them a pillow for my heart.
Augustine, *The Confessions*

The man and his wife were both naked, and they felt no shame.
Genesis 2:25

And they all deserted him and ran away. A young man followed with nothing on but a linen cloth. They caught hold of him, but he left the cloth in their hands and ran away naked.
Mark 14:50–52 (NJB)

Is this what the shame of Adam and Eve felt like? Here I crouch in the brush naked. I am frightened, and I wonder what they will do to me if they catch me. What about Him? What will that angry mob do to the Teacher? Why were they armed with clubs and swords?

Only a few short hours ago, the Teacher and His disciples met in a large upper room in our home for the Passover dinner. We considered it a great honor to host One so highly esteemed. My family had witnessed Him healing many tormented by disease. He taught in a way that captivated both Hebrew and Samaritan, rich and poor alike. But the same teachings that held us in a grip of grace seemed to infuriate the Pharisees, Sadducees, and elders. Yet, Jesus of Nazareth was unafraid of any who threatened Him.

We had prepared a beautiful seder meal for the wondrous honor of hosting this great Prophet during the holy days.

Late in the evening, after the Passover feast and the traditional singing of the Psalms, the Teacher and His disciples decided to walk to Gethsemane. I, on the other hand, retired for the evening. Removing my outer cloak, I quickly faded into a peaceful sleep.

A short time later, one of our servants awoke me in a state of alarm. A hostile crowd, led by one of Jesus' disciples, had come to our door demanding to arrest the Teacher. Panicked, the servant had sent them toward Gethsemane.

Realizing a great treachery was at hand, I rushed out of my home toward the garden to warn Him, wearing nothing but my nightclothes.

When I arrived, Jesus was being led away in irons. Were all His disciples a part of this ploy, or had they simply abandoned their Master in His peril?

I followed at a distance, trying to remain hidden in the shadows. But one of the soldiers must have caught sight of me. Two large hands came from behind and grabbed me by the collar. Releasing a scream, I tried to pull away, but the grip was too strong. All I could do was slip my body from my nightclothes and run for my life into the darkness.

I can hear their mocking laughter as they search for me in the garden.

So, I hide here, naked and afraid. My tears blind my vision. I am ashamed; ashamed of fleeing; ashamed of my fear; ashamed that I may never see the Teacher again. Will these tears ever end?

Lord Jesus Christ, have mercy upon me.

This follower that ran away naked and ashamed loved You, Lord.
He invited You into his home,
allowing "the lamb that was slain from the foundation of eternity"
to have Passover with His disciples.
Later in the evening, upon learning of Your betrayal,
he ran to the garden. He wanted to warn You of the danger.
He even attempted to follow You in the shadows.
But when confronted by those that hated You, he fled.
Filled with fear and dread, he ran away, naked and ashamed.

Lord, I want "the lamb that was slain
from the foundation of eternity" to always reside in my heart.
There have been many times I have wanted to stand up
for truth and be bold in my faith.
But when confronted with a world that hates You,
I have often fled. Christ, I ask you to satisfy me with faith
and confidence. Before the enemy, clothe me with
the whole armor of God. But before You, Christ,
let me have a heart that is ever naked and never ashamed.

Lord Jesus Christ, have mercy upon me.

They made their hearts as hard as flint and would not listen to the law or to the words that the LORD Almighty had sent by his Spirit through the earlier prophets.

Zechariah 7:12

Hidden Trial

Here we may reign secure, and in my choyce
to reign is worth ambition though in Hell:
Better to reign in Hell, than serve in Heav'n.
Milton, *Paradise Lost*

Then the detachment of soldiers with its commander and the Jewish officials arrested Jesus. They bound him and brought him first to Annas, who was the father-in-law of Caiaphas, the high priest that year. Caiaphas was the one who had advised the Jews that it would be good if one man died for the people. Meanwhile, the high priest questioned Jesus about his disciples and his teaching. "I have spoken openly to the world," Jesus replied. "I always taught in synagogues or at the temple, where all the Jews come together. I said nothing in secret. Why question me? Ask those who heard me. Surely they know what I said." When Jesus said this, one of the officials nearby struck him in the face. "Is this the way you answer the high priest?" he demanded. "If I said something wrong," Jesus replied, "testify as to what is wrong. But if I spoke the truth, why do you strike me?" Then Annas sent him, still bound, to Caiaphas the high priest.

John 18:12–14, 19–24

As I recount this matter, I admittedly do so filled with a righteous anger at the obstinate false prophet that stood before our council a few minutes ago.

It was the darkest of nights as we brought the one they called Jesus before the true leader of Israel. You must understand why I call Annas the true leader. Ever since these bothersome Romans took control of our beloved land, they have worked hard to usurp the Almighty's established authority of the Jews. Annas, chosen by Quirinius over thirty years ago, is our high priest for life, for that is Jewish law. In this choice, we saw God's hand.

But typical to Roman fashion, he was removed only twenty-one years after his installment. The Romans are insidious about deposing our religious leaders when they become threatened by the power of Jewish authority. And of Annas, they should feel threatened, for he speaks as the oracles of God. His current successor is his son-in-law, Caiaphas. A God-fearing man, Caiaphas acknowledges Annas as the righteous authority behind the priesthood of Israel. Thus, when a question of grave importance arises, Annas (in secret) is the first to make judgment.

On this cold evening, we stood and observed our high priest question the false prophet, Jesus of Nazareth. During this hidden trial, we saw this dangerous man reveal his arrogance and disrespect for God's true authority. Out of the Nazarene's mouth spewed words that even caused Annas to cringe. "I always taught in synagogues or at the temple, where all the Jews come together. I said nothing in secret. Why question Me? Ask those who heard Me. Surely they know what I said."

Oh, the mockery of his little lecture enraged me! Our great leader must hide in the shadows while this usurper proclaims he teaches in public! He cut to the quick of Annas's heart. I could not stand by and listen to such smugness any longer. Though the prisoner was bound, I struck him hard in the face with my hand, drawing blood from his filthy lips. I know this to be an illegality of the court, but none chastised me, for they saw God's justice in my actions.

The detainee spoke to me. "If I said something wrong, testify as to what is wrong. But if I spoke the truth, why do you strike me?"

This man will pay the price of God's wrath! We need no witnesses or proof to justify our actions. He is a rebel and he will die for his defiant words.

Lord Jesus Christ, have mercy upon me.

I said to the Lord,
"So often I find myself hidden in the darkness."
And He replied, "Let me bring to light the hidden things of
darkness and reveal the counsels of your heart."
I again spoke.
"But Lord, there are hidden areas of darkness
even now in my heart."
And He replied,
"You no longer have fellowship with the unfruitful works of
darkness, but now expose them. For you were once in
darkness, but now you are light in the Lord.
Walk as a child of light."
One last time I spoke.
"How, Lord, do I remain light?"
With a smile He replied yet again,
"He who loves his brother abides in the light,
and there is no cause for stumbling in him."

Lord Jesus Christ, have mercy upon me.

Suppose I go to the Israelites and say to them,
"The God of your fathers has sent me to you," and they ask me,
"What is his name?"
Then what should I tell them?
God said to Moses,
"I AM WHO I AM."

Exodus 3:13-14

Sanhedrin

Why am I a Christian? . . . Jesus. Brilliant, untamed, tender, creative, slippery, irreducible, paradoxically humble—Jesus stands up to scrutiny. He is who I want my God to be.

Phillip Yancey, *The Jesus I Never Knew*

Those who had arrested Jesus took him to Caiaphas, the high priest, where the teachers of the law and the elders had assembled. The chief priests and the whole Sanhedrin were looking for false evidence against Jesus so that they could put him to death. But they did not find any. Many testified falsely against him, but their statements did not agree. Finally two came forward and declared, "This fellow said, 'I am able to destroy the temple of God and rebuild it in three days.'" Yet even then their testimony did not agree. Then the high priest stood up and said to Jesus, "Are you not going to answer? What is this testimony that these men are bringing against you?" But Jesus remained silent. The high priest said to him, "I charge you under oath by the living God: Tell us if you are the Christ, the Son of God." "I am." Jesus replied. "But I tell all of you: In the future you will see the Son of Man sitting at the right hand of the Mighty One and coming on the clouds of heaven." Then the high priest tore his clothes and said, "He has spoken blasphemy! Why do we need any more witnesses? Look, now you have heard the blasphemy. What do you think?" "He is worthy of death," they answered. Then they spit in his face [blindfolded him] and struck him with their fists. Others slapped him and said, "Prophesy to us, Christ. Who hit you?" And the guards took him and beat him.

Matthew 26:57, 59–68 and Mark 14:56, 59, 62, 65

From the beginning this was nothing but a fool's theatre. The stage was set to give the appearance of legality during a morning of constant improprieties. The verdict had been cast days before. All the plans had neatly fallen into place until the actual trial. That is when things went wildly askew.

The delay of the pretrial before Annas had allowed Caiaphas to gather many of the seventy-one Sanhedrin. Those who had plotted this intricate deception had to find a legal basis to condemn their prisoner to death. Their most crucial witness, Judas Iscariot, had disappeared, so they had to quickly produce some witnesses.

Many came forward. Every one of them disagreed with the testimonies that preceded. It would have been laughable had it not been such a grave decision.

Finally, when two came forward declaring that Jesus said He would tear down the temple and rebuild it in three days, it was enough for Caiaphas. He had to get control of this madhouse. He once again questioned the man in chains.

Jesus had not been officially charged, so He allowed no answer to come forth. There would only be one thing that would bring the accused to words.

Caiaphas, in all his sanctimonious authority, charged the prisoner, by sacred oath, to answer this question: "Tell us if you are the Christ, the Son of God."

For the first time in the whole ridiculous procession, He looked up and spoke with unhindered conviction: "I am."

This reply, stunning the Sanhedrin into a split second of silence, had not been uttered for fifteen hundred years. They all knew it from their youngest childhood teachings. This declaration was ingrained into their psyche.

As they stood before the condemned man, His answer carried them back to the desert prophet who stood before a burning bush. "When I go before the Israelites and say the God of their Fathers sent me to you, who shall I say you are?" "I am . . ."

There was no more doubt; Jesus had openly declared His claim as the Christ. Caiaphas, in his rejection of the Messiah King, tore his clothes. Even though it was illegal, the punishment would begin now, as dark entities gathered into the men that stood around the Son of God. He was blindfolded and they began to mercilessly beat Him . . . yet he never uttered a sound. The "I am" would allow this drama to continue to unfold.

Lord Jesus Christ, have mercy upon me.

Lord, hear my cry:
This world is full of false accusers
and those who are indifferent to You.
Daily I battle with doubts, fears, and trials.
And if that was not enough,
there is an enemy that battles for my soul.
What am I to do?

Child, hear my declaration:
If your accusers surround you and speak wounding lies,
know that I AM your justice.
When you battle with your doubts and fears cloud your mind,
know that I AM your courage.
As you walk through trials of any degree,
know that I AM your strength.
And if the enemy comes against you like a flood,
know that I AM your shield.
I AM your Savior. I AM the Christ. I AM that I AM.

Lord, I believe. Take away my unbelief.

Lord Jesus Christ, have mercy upon me.

Strike the shepherd
and the sheep will be
scattered.

Zechariah 13:7

Denied

. . . repelling the hand that meant to loose my bonds, as though it only rubbed my sores.

Augustine, *The Confessions*

"I tell you the truth," Jesus answered, "this very night, before the rooster crows, you will disown me three times." But Peter declared, "Even if I have to die with you, I will never disown you."
Matthew 26:34–35

But Peter followed Him at a distance, right up to the courtyard of the high priest. He entered and sat down with the guards to see the outcome. A servant girl (when she saw Peter warming himself, she looked closely at him) came to him. "You were also with Jesus of Galilee," she said. But he denied it before them all. "I don't know what you're talking about," he said. Then he went out to the gateway, where another girl saw him and said to the people there, "This fellow was with Jesus of Nazareth." He denied it again, with an oath: "I don't know the man!" . . . "Surely you are one of them, for your (Galilean) accent gives you away." One of the high priest's servants, a relative of the man whose ear Peter had cut off, challenged him. "Didn't I see you with him in the olive grove?" Then he began to call down curses on himself and he swore to them, "I don't know the man!" Immediately a rooster crowed. Then Peter remembered the word Jesus had spoken: "Before the rooster crows, you will disown me three times." And he went outside and wept bitterly.
Matthew 26:58, 69–75; Mark 14:67, 70; and John 18:26

Where is the brave and brash Peter now? Who is this one that so freely swings a sword against an unarmed servant, but flees from the accusations of a little girl? How was I to know, Lord? Why have I run? How could I have denied You? Oh, what a wretched man I am!

He spoke to me a few hours ago with pity in His voice, revealing my denial. "Never my Lord! Even if all others walk away from You . . . Even if I have to die with You, I will never disown You!" The passion and resolve in my heart was genuine. Yet in Gethsemane could I not even pray for Him?

When the mob arrived at the garden, I lifted the sword in defense of Israel's Messiah. (Is that not odd to believe I could protect the Savior of Israel?) I was sure angels would charge to our righteous battle. Instead, He rebuked my rash act of anger. He did not resist that midnight injustice. Why did He act as if He was in control? Why did He not do anything? When I realized He would offer no resistance, I became bewildered. And in that moment of doubt, I ran and hid.

I finally mustered up enough courage to follow the procession to the courtyard of the high priest. I had to know what would happen to my friend, my Rabbi, my Lord. When the little girl approached me by the fire about being one of His followers, I was filled with dread. And what brave words did Petros proclaim from his lips? "I don't know what you're talking about."

I grew more uncomfortable as curious eyes started to read the denial on my face. I quickly made my way out of the courtyard to the front gate. The doorkeeper, a mere wisp of a girl, also took notice. "This fellow was with Jesus of Nazareth." How easy the frustrating falsehood of innocence jumped from my lips. "I don't know the man!"

But in my reckless rejection of Jesus, my thick country accent revealed the truth. That is when a witness to my garden bloodshed had no more doubt of my identity and asked, "Didn't I see you with him in the olive grove?" I exploded in a final tirade. "I don't know the man!"

At that moment my guilt, condemnation, and worst fear were loosed in the crow of a rooster. But I did not hear the bird. Instead, I heard His voice. "Who do you say I am, Simon Peter?" "You are the Christ, the Son of the Living God."

My Lord, what have I done? How could I so easily turn away? Have mercy upon me, Son of God!

Lord Jesus Christ, have mercy upon me.

This disciple of Yours, Peter, gave up everything to follow You.
He dropped his nets to become a fisher of men.
For three years, he followed You wherever You went.
He heard You in the temple and He saw You set men free.
He walked on water when You called,
and was there when You were gloriously transfigured.
And he declared, before all others, that
You are the Christ, Son of the Living God!
Still, he disowned You.
Yet, Jesus, You never let him go. Even in his darkest denial,
when he turned his back on You,
You never stopped loving him.
Lord, there are times I have disowned You in front of others.
There I times I have not stood as Your disciple.
Forgive me for the times I have disowned You in front of
men and for the times when no one is watching.
Jesus, allow Your Holy Spirit to fill me with a boldness
that allows me to lift You up.
Help me to live a life worthy of the calling I have received.
May I never disown You in my words, lifestyle, or actions.

Lord Jesus Christ, have mercy upon me.

He was despised and rejected
by men, a man of sorrows,
and familiar with suffering.
Like one from whom men
hide their faces
he was despised,
and we esteemed him not.

Isaiah 53:3

Pilate

IX

> *The fault-finder will find faults even in paradise.*
> **Henry David Thoreau, *Walden***

Very early in the morning, the chief priests, with the elders, the teachers of the law and the whole Sanhedrin reached a decision [to put Jesus to death]. They bound Jesus, led him away [to the palace of the Roman governor] and handed him over to Pilate. To avoid ceremonial uncleanness the Jews did not enter the palace; they wanted to be able to eat the Passover. So Pilate came out to them and asked, "What charges are you bringing against this man?" "If he were not a criminal," they replied, "we would not have handed him over to you." Pilate said, "Take him yourselves and judge him by your own law." "But we have no right to execute anyone," the Jews objected. This happened so that the words Jesus had spoken indicating the kind of death he was going to die would be fulfilled. [Jesus stood before the governor]. "Are you the king of the Jews?" asked Pilate. "Yes, it is as you say," Jesus replied. The chief priests accused him of many things. So again Pilate asked him, "Aren't you going to answer? See how many things they are accusing you of." But Jesus still made no reply, and Pilate was amazed.

Mark 15:1–5 and John 18:28–32

Pontius Pilate, Prefect of the Judean Province, to Herod Antipas, Tetrarch of Galilee, greetings:

As you know, though my usual dwelling is in Caesarea, I have temporarily taken residence in Jerusalem until the end of the Jewish holy day activities. The residents of Jerusalem have been very difficult as of late, and I believe my show of force during this period may quell any possible hidden rebellions. Order will be maintained amongst this markedly troublesome people of the Empire.

Early this morning, a large number of the Jewish Council awoke me from my chambers, demanding to speak with me. Of course, not wanting to defile their precious selves in the home of a "pagan" ruler, they insisted on holding a most unusual trial in my courtyard. I must say, I was none too happy to be aroused from my slumber, but curiosity brought me before them.

They had in custody one called Jesus, a Nazarene, who has been causing quite a stir in the land the last few months. His face was severely swollen from an apparent mete of justice these leaders had already taken into their own hands—a serious impropriety for sure. Many charges had been brought against him; I believe all of them to be absurd. But there was one charge he answered to that brings me some concern. I asked him if he claimed, as his enemies stated, to be the "king of the Jews." His answer was cryptic. He said, "It is as you say."

In asking his accusers for more information, I readily have come to this conclusion: to these incommodious troublemakers, I am nothing more than an executioner's pawn in their jealous schemes against this Jesus, whom I may find a bit fanatical but certainly not dangerous. They are hypocrites planning a man's murder, yet refusing to be ritually unclean because of my presence.

I am not impressed with their charge of blasphemy. So if it is a game they want to play, then let them play it before the proper Galilean authority.

With that said, I send you this most unusual indictment to decide upon as you see fit. May you judge with more patience than I am willing to give to these ridiculous charges.

In the name of our most excellent Lord, Tiberius, Caesar of the Roman Empire, good morrow.

Lord Jesus Christ, have mercy upon me.

Jesus, they dragged You before the rulers of this world.
Hatred fueled their accusations.
Jealousy and envy drove their ambition.
Yet You remained silent to all their lies.
But this one charge You answered.
"Are you the King of the Jews?"
And You replied: "Yes, it is as you say."
Do I believe that You are my sovereign king?
Do I believe that the rulers of this world are ultimately
under Your rule?
Do I believe that the enemies of God cannot go beyond
the boundaries of Your judgment?
Do I allow You to rule and reign in my life?
Do I give You the right to rule the kingdom of my heart?
Lord, show me the inner sanctuary of my mind and thoughts
so I can honestly answer these questions.

Lord Jesus Christ, have mercy upon me.

The kings of the **earth** take their **stand** and the **rulers** gather together **against** the **LORD** and against **his Anointed One.**

Psalm 2:2

Herod

I am trying here to prevent anyone saying the really foolish thing that people often say about Him: 'I'm ready to accept Jesus as a great moral teacher, but I don't accept His claim to be God.' That is the one thing we must not say. A man who was merely a man and said the sort of things Jesus said would not be a great moral teacher. He would either be a lunatic—on a level with the man who says he is a poached egg— or else he would be the Devil of Hell. You must make your choice. Either this man was, and is, the Son of God: or else a madman or something worse. You can shut Him up for a fool, you can spit at Him and kill Him as a demon; or you can fall at His feet and call Him Lord and God. But let us not come with any patronising nonsense about His being a great human teacher. He has not left that open to us. He did not intend to.

C. S. Lewis, *Mere Christianity*

When Herod saw Jesus, he was greatly pleased, because for a long time he had been wanting to see him. From what he had heard about him, he hoped to see him perform some miracle. He plied him with many questions, but Jesus gave him no answer. The chief priests and the teachers of the law were standing there, vehemently accusing him. Then Herod and his soldiers ridiculed and mocked him. Dressing him in an elegant robe, they sent him back to Pilate. That day Herod and Pilate became friends—before this they had been enemies.

Luke 23:8–12

Herod Antipas, Tetrarch of Galilee and Perea, to Pontius Pilate, Most Excellent Prefect of the Judean Province, greetings:

I have attempted to interrogate the prisoner you so graciously sent to me for judgment. When I received your letter, I was overjoyed for the opportunity to observe this miracle man from Galilee. In fact, I have been anxious for an audience with this Jesus ever since I learned that he was cousin to that troublesome desert nomad, John the Baptist. As you know, John was in my custody until his unfortunate death.

Though his accusers claim that this Jesus does not think much of me (for he refers to me as a "fox"), I was hoping he would perform some of his miraculous magic tricks and prove himself the prophet others claim him to be. Instead, he has turned out to be as troublesome and arrogant as his deceased cousin was to me a few months ago. I posed multiple questions to him, but in mockery directed at my authority, he stayed utterly mute. He may be a great teacher to the common people, but he is no prophet and certainly no king to the Jews.

In return for his contempt toward me, I have decided to dole out derision toward his outrageous claims. I must thank you for allowing us this sport at the beginning of the holy days. I could not have imagined I would find so much enjoyment in this surprise trial. With that in mind, and because he refused to defend any of the claims against him, I have returned the prisoner to you. The game is once again in your hands. Enjoy this well-dressed king that returns to your courts and greet him like the messiah he claims to be—or condemn him to death. It makes no difference to me.

I look forward to our next reunion and I hope to join you for a meal shortly after the holy days.

May you prosper much under the all-seeing eye of the Roman Empire.

Lord Jesus Christ, have mercy upon me.

Jesus, I cannot endure when they mock You, my Lord.
The enemies of God are forever in derision toward Your name.
They may call You a miracle worker.
They may call You a wise teacher.
They may even call You a benevolent prophet.
And most call You a good man.

But You are God.

Your Word proclaims,
"If you lift Me up, I will draw all men unto Me."
Teach me to lift You up in my actions and in my countenance.
Show me how to lift You up in front of
family, friends, and strangers alike.
Let the Spirit of Christ shine so authentically from me that
no one I meet will call You anything else but Lord and
Savior.

Lord Jesus Christ, have mercy upon me.

I have
chosen the way of truth;
I have set my heart
on your laws.
I hold fast to your
statutes, O LORD;
do not let me be put to shame.

Psalm 119:30-31

Truth

Have no fear in pursuing truth, wherever it takes you. Because our fundamental conviction is that God is the God of truth. If you find truth, God is going to be there.

Simone Neil

Pilate then went back inside the palace, summoned Jesus and asked him, "Are you the king of the Jews?" "Is that your own idea," Jesus asked, "or did others talk to you about me?" "Am I a Jew?" Pilate replied. "It was your people and your chief priests who handed you over to me. What is it you have done?" Jesus said, "My kingdom is not of this world. If it were, my servants would fight to prevent my arrest by the Jews. But now my kingdom is from another place." "You are a king, then!" said Pilate. Jesus answered, "You are right in saying I am a king. In fact, for this reason I was born, and for this I came into the world, to testify to the truth. Everyone on the side of truth listens to me." "What is truth?" Pilate asked.

John 18:33–38

Pilate called together the chief priests, the rulers and the people, and said to them, "You brought me this man as one who was inciting the people to rebellion. I have examined him in your presence and have found no basis for your charges against him. Neither has Herod, for he sent him back to us; as you can see, he has done nothing to deserve death. Therefore, I will punish him and then release him."

Luke 23:13–16

The accusations against the Christ were nothing short of ludicrous deceptions created by a jealous group of religious leaders hell-bent on holding power in their clutches. But the influence of these lies came from a much more insidious source. He had met this source ere the beginning of creation.

The one determined to see the Messiah crushed had taken a multitude of disguises throughout the ages. He had posed as an alluring serpent in Eden and successfully seduced mankind into slavery. In the courts of heaven, he argued for the soul of Job as a brilliant but untriumphant prosecutor. Three years ago, he had faced this Jesus once again, unsuccessfully attempting to bait Him into the miscarriage of His mission. And now this foe of old had his prey where he wanted Him. Or so he thought . . .

The deceptive and contrary nature of these charges had sent this nomadic court case from one location to another. The house of Annas and Caiaphas; the courtyard of Pilate; the palace of Herod; and finally back to Pilate's court. The disregard for proper justice was dizzying. It was clear to Pilate that this man posed no threat. He saw himself as a king of some sort, but he clearly portrayed his reign as spiritual in nature.

Yet the one point that disturbed Pilate was this regal Jew's claim to be an ambassador of truth. Not a representative of a truth, but a Truth that was the source of all that is good, right, and real. Pilate's Roman sensibilities would not allow him to even consider the possibility of a single source of Truth. Truth was what every man deemed for himself, and if necessary, truth was what the strongest demanded it be.

In the naivete of his youth, when Pilate foolishly believed in goodness, he had considered this possibility. But the cruelty of life had taught him otherwise. The presence of this man, however, caused his own sensibilities to crumble. Before he could think it through, he uttered a most dangerous statement: "What is truth?" This declaration was safe in the classroom of pondering philosophy students, but in the presence of Jesus it was cataclysmic. And for Pilate, it was too much.

Pilate called the mob of religious leaders together. "I have examined him in your presence and have found no basis for your charges against him. He has done nothing to deserve death. Therefore, I will punish him and then release him."

But the enemy of Truth would not allow his prey so easy an escape.

Lord Jesus Christ, have mercy upon me.

I ask you, Lord, who may dwell in Your sanctuary?
Your Word proclaims:
He whose walk is blameless and who does what is righteous.
Who speaks the truth from his heart.
Teach me Your way, O Lord, and I will walk in Your name.
Show me Your ways, O Lord, teach me Your paths;
Guide me in Your truth and teach me,
For You are my God and my Savior,
And my hope is in You all day long.
Send forth Your light and Your truth, let them guide me;
Let them bring me to Your holy mountain,
To the place You dwell.
Teach me Your way, O Lord, That I can walk in Your truth.
Give me an undivided heart That I may fear Your name.

Lord Jesus Christ, have mercy upon me.

I have **swept away**
your offenses like a cloud,
your **sins**
like the **morning mist.**
Return to me,
for I have **redeemed** you.

Isaiah 44:22

Barabbas

Alexander, Caesar, Charlemagne, and myself founded empires; but upon what . . . ? Jesus Christ alone founded His empire upon love; and at this hour millions would die for Him.

Napoleon Bonaparte

Now it was the governor's custom at the Feast to release a prisoner whom the people requested. A man called Barabbas was in prison with the insurrectionists who had committed murder in the uprising. The crowd came up and asked Pilate to do for them what he usually did. While Pilate was sitting on the judge's seat, his wife sent him this message: "Don't have anything to do with that innocent man, for I have suffered a great deal today in a dream because of him." But the chief priests and the elders persuaded the crowd to ask for Barabbas and to have Jesus executed. "Do you want me to release to you the king of the Jews?" asked Pilate, knowing it was out of envy that the chief priests had handed Jesus over to him. But the chief priests stirred up the crowd to have Pilate release Barabbas instead.

Mark 15:6–11 and Matthew 27:15–21

Righteous Lord, I sit here in this prison cell awaiting my martyrdom. Even now, I hear the people screaming my name. "Barabbas! Give us Barabbas!" They want my blood because they don't understand. In a few moments, I will carry a cross for what I believe and have given my life. May that cross clench their dull and fearful minds. Let them always remember that I am a freedom fighter even though they label me a insurrectionist and murderer. I have been a faithful Zealot, devoted to Your ways and walking in the footsteps of my fathers. You know Lord, like Elijah and Phinehas of old, I stood in defiance of these pagan conquerors. Unlike our apathetic religious leaders, I refused to pay tribute to these Roman pigs! You are my King and the only One worthy of tribute. Rebellion to these tyrants is obedience to You! May my death stir up Your chosen people to oppose these hell-bound dictators of the Jews. I proudly go to this honored death. I know You will reward me for every Roman soldier's neck I have cut. They don't even deserve to have their tainted blood spill on this holy land. Forgive me for every Jew that lost his life to a Roman because of my knife. May you take into consideration all the good I've done . . .

Two soldiers march to the front of his cell. "Barabbas! Time to go, you dog." As they release him from his chains, he spits in their faces with insolent poison of rebellion and hate. "You'd better settle down, you idiot, or you won't go free."

"Free? What do you mean? I am to die!" says the confused prisoner.

"Not today, you lucky piece of dung. The mob has demanded your release. Your Jewish 'holy man,' the Nazarene, will be taking your place." And with that, Barabbas is thrown to the streets—free to go.

I know of this man! One of our own, Simon, gave up his call as a Zealot to follow him. Why has Jesus done this? Why does he now take my place in execution? Do the people hate him so much? What has he done to deserve death? Oh Lord, what have I done? I deserved this death—even craved it! Where will I go and what will I do? This innocent man will be carrying my cross . . . my cross! He is like a lamb to the slaughter. Why have You allowed him to pay for my death?

Lord Jesus Christ, have mercy upon me.

So many times when the clouds of confusion
clear from my mind, I find I am in a dark, lonely prison cell
awaiting judgment. The walls of this jail are self-imposed,
built by me a stone at a time.
On careful examination, I realize these walls
are constructed of such things
as the bitter disappointments of my unfulfilled expectations,
buried anger I often harbor toward people,
the blindness of my selfish desires,
and my willing seduction by the things of this world.
These stones turn out to be carefully placed and
mortared by my prideful heart and purposed ignorance.
Then You arrive and burst open my prison doors.
You proclaim, "Come forward, for I have set you free!
If you will only confess your sins,
I will be faithful and just to forgive all your trespasses."
You throw my sin as far as the east is from the west
and my burdens are lifted.
Help me, Jesus, to never build those prison walls again.
And if, by chance, I begin to build the walls of this prison,
let Your Word come in like a wrecking ball
to demolish all I have assembled.

Lord Jesus Christ, have mercy upon me.

All a man's ways
seem right to him, but
the LORD weighs the heart.
To do what is right and just is
more acceptable to the
LORD than sacrifice.

Proverbs 21:2-3

Condemned

I expect to pass through this world but once; any good thing therefore that I can do, or any kindness I can show to any fellow creature, let me do it now; let me not defer or neglect it, for I shall not pass this way again.

Stephen Grellet

Wanting to release Jesus, Pilate appealed to them again. "What shall I do, then, with Jesus who is called the Christ?" Pilate asked. They all answered, "Crucify him!" "Why? What crime has he committed? I have found in him no grounds for the death penalty. Therefore I will have him punished and then release him," [said Pilate.] But they shouted all the louder and insistently demanded, "Crucify him!" . . . and their shouts prevailed. When Pilate saw that he was getting nowhere, but that instead an uproar was starting, Pilate decided to grant their demand. He took water and washed his hands in front of the crowd. "I am innocent of this man's blood," he said. "It is your responsibility!" All the people answered, "Let his blood be on us and our children!" And [he] surrendered Jesus to their will.

Matthew 27:22–25 and Luke 23:20–25

This was his last chance to bring an end to the madness of this twisted morning. This strange type of ordeal was the very source of Pilate's hatred for being posted in this ghetto on the edge of the Empire. He despised these people, and more so, their manipulative leaders.

For the first time in his Palestinian military career, he had met an honorable and worthy Jew. And what was he about to do? He was going to give into the demands of these angry puppeteers that were pulling his bureaucratic strings. He released a dangerous insurrectionist who had murdered many of his own military and would now execute an innocent and peaceful man.

But Pilate would try one last option. Certainly the common people, who had now gathered as a multitude in his courtyard, would let this Jesus go after a lesser punishment. "Whom do I release?"

But only one response poured forth from their throats: "CRUCIFY HIM!"

"But he has committed no crime."

"CRUCIFY HIM!"

The shouts reminded him of a time when, as a little boy, he had witnessed a gladiator fight. One of the combatants had beaten his weakened opponent into a crouched position. The vanquished warrior muttered one word to his opponent: "Mercy . . ." Pilate recalled the crowd falling into a wild frenzy and shrieking as one voice over and over: "KILL! KILL! KILL! KILL!" Pilate felt as if he was reliving that childhood nightmare again.

"CRUCIFY HIM!"

This battle was also lost, yet the victim did not cry for mercy. The captive Jesus looked upon the homicidal crowd with what seemed to be pity, and dare Pilate think, affection.

Pilate could not afford another embarrassing riot. He would allow this travesty of judgment. But Pilate had one more act of protest to carry out.

Quieting the agitated assembly, Pilate had a Jewish ceremonial washbasin brought before him. The curiously hushed rabble now watched this pagan ruler ceremonially wash his hands like a pious Jew. On this day, of all days, they knew the significance of that action. Pilate was brashly declaring that he would not accept the blame of this man's blood on his head. He would not take responsibility of the cross Jesus would soon bear.

Defiantly they reacted, "Let his blood be upon us and our children!"

Lord Jesus Christ, have mercy upon me.

If your love for earthly relationships is greater than your love
for Me
You are not worthy of Me.

Help me, Jesus, to love You above all others.

If you wash your hands of the responsibility of the cross and
following Me
You are not worthy of Me.

Help me, Jesus, to pick up the cross and follow You
anywhere You lead.

If you seek for your well-being alone,
you will lose yourself on the way.

Help me, Jesus, to lay my life down.

But if you sacrifice your life for My sake
you will find an abundant life.

Thank you, Christ, for abundant life.

Lord Jesus Christ, have mercy upon me.

Then Pilate
took Jesus
and had him
[scourged].

John 19: 1

Scourge

[When you pass from this world into eternity] God will not look you over for medals, degrees or diplomas, but for scars.
Elbert Hubbard

I offered my back to those who beat me, my cheeks to those who pulled out my beard; I did not hide my face from mocking and spitting.
Isaiah 50:6

Wanting to satisfy the crowd, Pilate released Barabbas to them.
Mark 15:15

Pilate's last attempt to appease the crowd took place in the form of the scourge; perhaps a generous show of blood would be enough meted punishment. This noble Jew would certainly be severely scarred for the rest of his life, but he would stay alive, and that was something.

Every male convicted to execution under Roman law was required to endure the scourge before the final torture. Many prisoners, if fortunate, died under the whip before they ever made it to the cross.

After stripping Jesus to a loincloth, the soldiers led Him to the post in the middle of Pilate's courtyard. At the top of the post a ring was mounted with a rope dangling through it. Securely tying His hands with the cord, the soldiers pulled Jesus' body up toward the ring until He stood upon the tips of His toes. The powerful frame of the Carpenter was stretched taut. Every muscle and every sinew was defined on His extended body. If not for the obvious posture of torture, one would have been reminded of an ancient Greek statue reaching to the heavens.

The guard who administered the lashes was an expert at the scourge. He was painfully accurate and his tool was no mere whip. It was designed to inflict the most punishing wounds possible. Three leather cords hung from the handle. Each cord was studded with bone and metal fragments that would act as hooks. This punishment consisted of thirteen lashes. Pilate had ordered the guard to ". . . make it appear as horrible as possible but spare the life of this Jew."

Once Jesus was in position, the skilled punisher took a moment to study his victim's body. He dipped the scourge into a basin of warm water so the leather would adhere to the skin. Standing behind his target, he aimed for the mid-back. Slash! As the cords wrapped around Jesus' powerful frame, the bone and the metal at the tips of the leather sunk into His body. Feeling the hook, the guard turned himself around, twisting the cords. The hooks gripped into Jesus' flesh. With all his strength, the punisher pulled away. He stood somewhat stunned as his victim let out a lone muffled moan. Up to this point in his ghastly career, there had always been screams. He had torn three twelve-inch strips of flesh from the man's body, yet Jesus barely moved. He repeated this process for several minutes until thirty-nine stripes had been filleted from the prisoner's neck to His calves. Victim and torturer stood crimson. Lacerations covered Jesus' frame, yet He never cried for mercy.

As they cut his body down, the torturer wondered, "Who is this man?"

Lord Jesus Christ, have mercy upon me.

You were pierced for our transgressions and
crushed for our iniquities.
Your punishment brought us peace and by Your stripes
. . . blind eyes open, unbreakable hearts break,
and stubborn ways change.
. . . Gentiles acquire hope, the worthless become priceless,
and the poor are wealthy.
. . . foolish assumptions expire, blind faith becomes
unnecessary, and man's wisdom hollows.
. . . Babylon's call is muted, the yoke of bondage cracked,
and the mark of Cain disappears.
. . . consuming fears take flight, destructive words shatter,
and hatred loses all its power.
. . . eternal separation becomes endless reunion,
idols are destroyed, and the curtain is torn.
. . . the debts of our past are paid, the law fulfilled,
and a King sits on the throne.
. . . sickness is healed, pain is swallowed in joy,
and sorrow fills with laughter.
. . . man is restored, nakedness is covered,
and Passover is concluded.
. . . the rocks cry out, creation groans,
and devils continue to tremble.
. . . enemies are reconciled, the lost are saved,
and tongues are loosed.
. . . Adam's sin is redeemed, the seduction of the world fades,
and the devil's grasp loosens.
. . . hell is defeated, death loses its sting,
and the grave remains empty.

Lord Jesus Christ, have mercy upon me.

Just as there were many
who were appalled at him—
his appearance was so
disfigured
beyond that of any man
and his form marred
beyond human likeness.

Isaiah 52:14

Crown

So Eden sank to grief,
So dawn goes down to day . . .
Robert Frost, "Nothing Gold Can Stay"

Then the governor's soldiers took Jesus into the Praetorium and gathered the whole company of soldiers around him. They stripped him and put a scarlet robe on him, and then twisted together a crown of thorns and set it on his head. They put a staff in his right hand and knelt in front of him and mocked him. "Hail, king of the Jews!" they said. They spit on him, and took the staff and struck him on the head again and again. (Falling on their knees, they paid homage to him). From then on, Pilate tried to set Jesus free, but the Jews kept shouting, "If you let this man go, you are no friend of Caesar. Anyone who claims to be a king opposes Caesar." When Pilate heard this, he brought Jesus out and sat down on the judge's seat at a place known as the Stone Pavement. It was the day of Preparation of Passover Week, about the sixth hour. "Here is your king," Pilate said to the Jews. But they shouted, "Take him away! Take him away! Crucify him!" "Shall I crucify your king?" Pilate asked. "We have no king but Caesar," the chief priests answered. After they had mocked him, they took off the robe and put his own clothes on him.
Matthew 27:27–31; Mark 15:19; and John 19:12–15

I tell you this account that you may clearly understand why I have asked for the relief of my commission. Though it is of minor importance, it may help you to know that I come from a noble Roman family in the seaport town of Troas on the eastern edge of Macedonia. My ancestors were a part of the royal guard that marched with Alexander the Great when this part of the world became a Greek city-state. You could say being a soldier is in my nature. But I no longer have the stomach nor the will to carry on this occupation of death.

My place in this tale begins in the Praetorium. Pilate had ordered me to oversee the execution of an innocent man. This man, Jesus the Nazarene, had somehow stirred the religious hornet's nest of the Sanhedrin. In some sort of political game of chaos, this dignified carpenter would receive the punishment set for a bloodthirsty assassin named Barabbas.

After his scourging, the prisoner was brought before several hundred soldiers, most of whom held a ferocious and ever-brewing contempt for this subject nation. These men had waited months to see Barabbas pay for the deaths of their brothers in arms. Now Barabbas was gone and this man was all we were left with. The charge of death was because of his supposed claim to be the king of the Jews.

Knowing the anger building in the company of soldiers, I decided to allow them to make sport of this one who would die very soon. The building pressure of the soldiers' lives would have to be appeased, or more senseless aggression would occur.

Removing his blood-soaked clothes, the men found a faded military cloak and placed it on his shoulders. One of the soldiers had collected a vine of wickedly long palm spines and created a makeshift crown. A rough-hewn scepter was placed into his right hand and many bowed, yelling, "Hail, king of the Jews!"

In a grotesque flash, they started to beat him senseless. Some pulled out chunks of his beard while others beat his already lacerated body and head with the stick. He was beaten until you could barely recognize him as human. All their fury was poured on this one man. Wonder of wonders—throughout the agonizing torture, the prisoner barely moaned. Pilate tried to release him again, but the crowd demanded blood.

I must rest, for I do not feel so well. Give me some time and I will tell you more of this sad tale.

Lord Jesus Christ, have mercy upon me.

They twisted a crown of thorns upon Your head
and called You a King.
And they were right.
You are a King, the King of Kings.
Help me, Jesus, to follow You in such a manner
that I will not be disqualified for the prize—
a crown that will last forever.
And may that crown be righteousness which the Lord,
the Righteous Judge will award to me on that day.
Then, as I one day approach Your throne,
allow me to lay down that crown
before Your feet and say,
"You are worthy, our Lord and our God,
to receive glory and honor and power,
for You created all things,
and by Your will they were created and have their being."

Lord Jesus Christ, have mercy upon me.

God himself will
provide the lamb
for the
burnt offering,
my son.

Genesis 22:8

The Cross

[Jesus was called to wear a cross but not a crown] . . . For Jesus to save others, quite simply, he could not save himself.
Phillip Yancey, *The Jesus I Never Knew*

Abraham took the wood for the burnt offering and placed it on his son Isaac, and he himself carried the fire and the knife. As the two of them went on together, Isaac spoke up and said to his father Abraham, "Father?" "Yes, my son?" Abraham replied. "The fire and wood are here," Isaac said, "but where is the lamb for the burnt offering?"
Genesis 22:6–7

After they had mocked him, they took off the robe and put his own clothes on him. Finally Pilate handed him over to them to be crucified. So the soldiers took charge of Jesus. Then they led him away to crucify him, . . . carrying his own cross.
Matthew 27:31 and John 19:16–17

They gathered from across the vast scope of creation. The instrument of mystery that lay hidden from before the birth of matter, time, and eternity was about to be uncovered. The Maker subdues the angelic beings that are ready to burst through the hidden realm to save the Son. They may observe, but they are not to interfere in any way. The Son of God must carry this weight on His own shoulders.

The Christ was barely recognizable. His body was covered with caustic bruises and great clots of blood. A large-framed soldier of eastern descent ripped the robe from His body, reopening the wounds that covered every inch of His frame. As the blood flowed from His torn flesh, the angelic beings gasped. Many of the invisible observers wept at the insanity displayed before them. The sweat, blood, and waste of the prisoner caused the air to grow pungent. The Son of God was clothed once again by a vulgar-mouthed guard who forced a bloodied garment back onto His trembling body. Two fellow prisoners were already on the execution road. Time was running short and the soldiers were growing impatient.

At this moment, all of heaven became immobilized. Deep within their spirits, they knew the mystery would now be revealed. What would the Son do? Would He call the angels to burst forth in a triumphant shout of judgment? Would the One they called Savior transfigure before His enemies and reveal His true self?

One cherubim broke the silence and pointed saying, "No! It cannot be. That cannot be the mystery. Not a cross!"

Forcing the Christ to His knees, two men plunged a rough-hewn crossbeam onto the Son's shoulders. The splinters dug deep into His back. Tying His arms to the crossbeam, the soldiers forced the Son to start the journey toward the appointed place of execution.

The angelic host watched His face. Grimacing at first, the Son stood exhausted. But an intense dignity was set in His brow. He would carry the instrument of His humiliation, torture, and death. All would think Him accursed by God.

So it was true. The will of the Father was something none of them had anticipated. God Himself had provided the Lamb for the sin offering. That offering would be His beloved Son.

Lord Jesus Christ, have mercy upon me.

When I survey the wondrous cross*
On which the Prince of glory died,
My richest gain I count but loss,
And pour contempt on all my pride.

Forbid it, Lord, that I should boast,
Save in the death of Christ my God!
All the vain things that charm me most,
I sacrifice them to His blood.

See from His head, His hands, His feet,
Sorrow and love flow mingled down!
Did e'er such love and sorrow meet,
Or thorns compose so rich a crown?

His dying crimson, like a robe,
Spreads o'er His body on the tree;
Then I am dead to all the globe,
And all the globe is dead to me.

Were the whole realm of nature mine,
That were a present far too small;
Love so amazing, so divine,
Demands my soul, my life, my all.

Lord Jesus Christ, have mercy upon me.

*Isaac Watts, *Hymns and Spiritual Songs*, 1707 Public Domain

But I am a worm
and not a man, scorned
by men and despised
by the people.
All who see me mock me;
they hurl insults,
shaking their heads.

Psalm 22:6-7

First Fall

It is certain because it is impossible.
Tertullian, *De Carne Christi*

Your attitude should be the same as that of Christ Jesus: Who, being in very nature God, did not consider equality with God something to be grasped, but made himself nothing, taking the very nature of a servant, being made in human likeness. And being found in appearance as a man, he humbled himself and became obedient to death—even death on a cross!

Philippians 2:5–8

The path to Golgotha, on any other day, would have been nothing more than a pleasant stroll through the bustling streets of David's City. But on this day, the trek would become the most grueling journey any man would ever take.

The One who now carried a hundred pounds of raw wood on His beaten and bloodied back also bore the sins of all mankind (past, present, and future) on His human frame. No other vessel but His could ever contain the blemish of Eden and the hope of heaven. He understood this day from before He had uttered "Let there be light!" Before eternity, He had chosen enfleshment and embraced Gethsemane. His face was set like flint as He moved step-by-step down the very road He had paved before time.

The odd parade of soldiers, criminals, Sanhedrin, and the Christ left the fortress and worked its way toward the city gates. The streets were filled with visiting Jews from every corner of the empire. During the Passover celebration, Jerusalem would swell to maximum capacity, for it was a Jew's responsibility to make it to the holy city to celebrate Passover at least once in a lifetime. Throughout the streets, men walked briskly toward the temple, bearing unblemished lambs upon their shoulders. Those lambs were soon to be sacrificed as covering for their family's sins.

Jerusalem was ablaze with thousands of voices humming in the atmosphere. This made the journey to the execution site particularly tense and slower than usual. The soldiers, already on edge, pushed the condemned like sheep to the slaughter. All they wanted was to finish this nasty business as soon as possible.

By this point, Jesus was exhausted from the loss of sleep, blood, and water. His feet became unsteady as He walked the stone-paved streets toward His final destination. Finally, trembling under the weight of the crossbeam, the Son of God succumbed to the weakness of His flesh and went down. Hands tied and unable to catch Himself, He fell hard upon His face. The pain was excruciating. Without a moment of relief, two guards grabbed the beam, lifting the bearer who was tied to it. His shoulders felt as if they would separate from His body. In that moment, He grew foggy and started to lose consciousness.

The gentle "baa" of a single sacrificial lamb broke through the turmoil of the moment, jarring the Son of God back to His senses. He would go forth and finish the work the Father had set before Him.

Lord Jesus Christ, have mercy upon me.

I desire, Lord, to know You
in the fellowship of Your sufferings.
I do not want to lift my head higher than Your laws,
nor attempt to become the master of another
through manipulation, haughtiness, unforgiveness,
control, or any other ways I may have created.
Instead, I want to take on the depiction of Incarnation.
I desire to serve mankind through serving You.
Help me to be humble enough to bear the weight
of the cross upon my shoulders.
In turn, I will die to myself and live for You.

Lord Jesus Christ, have mercy upon me.

Then Simeon blessed them and
said to Mary, his mother:

"This **child** is destined to **cause**
the **falling** and **rising** of many
in Israel, and to be a
sign that will be spoken against,
so that the **thoughts** of many **hearts**
will be **revealed**. And a **sword**
will **pierce** your own **soul** too."

Luke 2:34-35

Mother of God

Why do I feel a tear upon my cheek? Why does it taste bittersweet? Why is it that I can feel when you cry though you're not near for me to see, for me to hear? It's at a time like this that I have a somehow knowing that you are calling my name. And I answer! It seems in vain, but I'm compelled to answer just the same.

Irving Dotson Crabbe, "Tear"

Therefore the Lord himself will give you a sign: The virgin will be with child and will give birth to a son, and will call him Immanuel.

Isaiah 7:14

When he was twelve years old, they went up to the Feast, according to the custom. After the Feast was over, while his parents were returning home, the boy Jesus stayed behind in Jerusalem, but they were unaware of it. When they did not find him, they went back to Jerusalem to look for him. After three days they found him in the temple courts. . . . When his parents saw him, they were astonished. His mother said to him, "Son, why have you treated us like this? Your father and I have been anxiously searching for you." "Why were you searching for me?" he asked. "Didn't you know I had to be in my Father's house?" . . . his mother treasured all these things in her heart.

Luke 2:42–43, 45–46, 48–49, 51

She broke through the crowd in a desperate devotion that only a mother can understand. Very early in the morning, she was woken with the words, "They have taken Him." Her instincts told her to prepare for the worst. This was a moment she had known since the haunting words of Simeon were spoken, ". . . a sword will pierce your own soul."

Her Son had been arrested and none knew why. He had been held in Pilate's courtyard for quite a long time. She heard the crowds yelling, "Crucify!" Still, she would not allow herself to believe what she already knew in her heart. What is happening to Him? Why have they not released Him?

By the time the gates to the fortress had opened, she had been pushed to the back of a vast crowd of onlookers waiting for this gruesome parade. Two criminals passed the multitude of onlookers who shouted out curses at the crossbearers. When a third man appeared, a collective horrific gasp echoed. Taking the opportunity, Mary forced her way through the throng, many of whom were now retreating from the front.

A man, if you could call him that, was carrying a crossbeam and was heading in her direction. The garment he was wearing was soaked crimson in his own blood. His head, a mass of bruises and bumps, carried upon it a wicked crown created out of thorns.

Hope filled her as the gates closed behind him. Her son was not there. He must have been released and she simply could not see Him in the crowd.

As the maimed criminal came past her, He looked up and caught her eye.

Time stopped and all went deathly silent. It was as if the world contained only her and this shattered man. His gaze gave Him away. In this frozen moment, she saw the beautiful eyes of a newborn babe in her arms. She remembered how His gentle little hands reached for her mouth and she kissed them tenderly. She remembered her twelve-year-old son, sitting in the temple with elders and teachers. That day she had been so worried for His safety and irritated at His actions. But when she looked into His eyes there was a playful wisdom. "Why were you searching for me? Didn't you know I had to be in my Father's house?"

This mutilated figure was her beloved son. She screamed in horror, trying to reach Him, but an annoyed soldier simply held her back. Once again, she caught His eyes and knew He was about His Father's work.

Lord Jesus Christ, have mercy upon me.

I sit amazed, as I gaze upon my children,
wondering how the mother of God fulfilled her role.
What was her anguish, her pain?
She watched her son,
pondering many hidden secrets in her heart.
She knew Him as Jesus, Savior, Immanuel,
God Is With Us, and son.
She knew Him better than any other.
But did she have other dreams for Him?
Certainly she hoped for the best and
wanted to watch Him thrive and grow.
But Your plans for Him were already set and
she had to give Him back to You.

Help me understand, Lord, that I am simply a steward of
the lives of my children.
I look at them and ponder many hopes, dreams,
and desires for their lives.
Yet, I want nothing neither more nor less than
Your will for them.
Aid me in knowing when to protect and when to let go.
Teach me to raise them in the admonition of You.
Allow my life to draw them closer to Your heart.
And when the day comes, help me release them back to You.

Lord Jesus Christ, have mercy upon me.

I myself will tend my sheep
and have them lie down,
declares the Sovereign LORD.
I will search for the lost
and bring back the strays.

Ezekiel 34:15–16

Simon

A slight taste of knowing God, a brief glimpse of His face, is enough to send echoes of longing careening wildly toward the boundaries of our souls. Our hearts will resonate with the nature, presence and truth of Christ as they cannot with anything else. It is what we were created for. He is both our hunger and our sustenance, our answer and our longing.

Charlie Peacock

A certain man from Cyrene, Simon, the father of Alexander and Rufus, was passing by on his way in from the country, and they forced him to carry the cross [behind Jesus].

Mark 15:21

Greet Rufus, chosen in the Lord, and his mother, who has been a mother to me, too.

Romans 16:13

Many have asked why my father gave himself to martyrdom. If you listen I will now tell you the simple, true tale of an encounter with a crossbearer and how it turned our lives in a direction we never contemplated.

Our family originated from a Jewish colony in the coastal city of Cyrene in North Africa. We were cultured, wealthy, intellectual, and known for our piety.

My grandfather, Simon, took my father, Rufus, and his brother, Alexander, to Jerusalem to celebrate the Passover. Can you imagine the excitement over a journey of that magnitude? Visiting the City of David on the holiest day of the year was the adventure of a lifetime. The voyage took several days by sea, and by the time they arrived, the city was filled to capacity. Instead, they stayed a few miles outside of Jerusalem in the surrounding country.

On the morning of Preparation, they started early toward Jerusalem so as to enjoy as much of the day's festivities as possible and to take a sacrifice to the temple. But the greeting they received at the gates of the city was anything but joyful. According to Uncle Alexander, an angry and menacing crowd was congested just inside the gates. As they entered, they found themselves staring at three men bearing patibulum (crossbeams) on their backs. Here, on the holiest of days, people were screaming for the sacrifice of these men.

One of the men, a thief, scowled and cursed the crowd. The second, also a thief, seemed distressed and he openly wept. My father always told me that the last man was too horrible to describe.

Grandfather often said that he immediately knew it could only have been God who sustained Him with the strength to walk with the cross. It was at that critical moment that Grandfather met the Lamb of God. The one-hundred-pound crossbeam on the third man's back had taken its toll and He started to stumble. A centurion caught Him and, in what Grandfather perceived to be an act of kindness, cut Him loose of the beam. "You! Get over here!" Simon was stunned but quick enough to tell his sons to follow closely.

My father said he thought my grandfather was about to be killed. Little did he know he was about to come alive! What happened after that will stay within our family. But I will tell you this. The words that the Christ spoke to my grandfather as he took the weight of the cross forever changed him and our family. They were words to live for and words worthy of dying for.

Lord Jesus Christ, have mercy upon me.

He came to worship, not knowing what to expect.
He was simply caught up in the holidays.
But on his way toward tradition, he met You face to face.
It was at this point that Simon became a crossbearer.
And as he took that cross upon his shoulders,
You whispered something in his ear.
Those few words of intimacy forever changed his life
and the lives of his children.

Jesus, many times I find myself caught up in the
tradition of worship.
But the only time worship results in transcendence
is when I meet You face to face.
As I carry the cross and follow You,
whisper words in my ears that will forever change me,
my children, and any I may touch with my life.

Lord Jesus Christ, have mercy upon me.

Is **not** this the kind of fasting
I have chosen:
to loose the **bonds** of injustice and
untie the cords of the yoke
to set the oppressed **free**
and **break** every yoke?
Is it **not** to **share** food with the
hungry and to provide the poor
wanderer with shelter—when you
see the naked, to **clothe** him?

Isaiah 58:6-7

Veronica

How can they meet us face to face till we have faces?
C. S. Lewis, *Till We Have Faces*

As Jesus was on his way, the crowds almost crushed him. And a woman was there who had been subject to bleeding for twelve years, but no one could heal her. She came up behind him and touched the edge of his cloak. She said to herself, "If I only touch his cloak, I will be healed." And immediately her bleeding stopped. "Who touched me?" Jesus asked. When they all denied it, Peter said, "Master, the people are crowding and pressing against you." But Jesus said, "Someone touched me; I know that power has gone out from me." Then the woman, seeing that she could not go unnoticed, came trembling and fell at his feet. In the presence of all the people, she told why she had touched him and how she had been instantly healed. Then he said to her, "Daughter, your faith has healed you. Go in peace."

Luke 8:42–48 and Matthew 9:21

The temporary relief of weight allowed the Son of God a brief respite. He was now heading downhill through the Valley of Tyropean. The hills of crucifixion appeared through His misty, blood-tainted sight. Lingering at the edge of the crowd since His exit from the fortress, a woman waited for just the right moment. There would be only one chance, and this faith-filled follower of the Healer would not waste it on a useless attempt. She must reach Him and touch His face. His bloodied body reminded her of the blood-debt that compelled her forward.

Her name was Veronica, but for years she was known as "Unclean." As a young woman, the starting of her menstrual cycle signaled her arrival into womanhood. But that which should have been a season of celebration turned into a twelve-year nightmare. Her cycle never stopped. She would sometimes flow blood for days, leaving her body drained of all strength. Many times during her life, she could not leave the confines of her home. The embarrassment of a sudden flow in public had been devastating the few times it happened. All the wealth her parents had left for her was spent on doctors who could not heal her.

But the most distressing aspect of her ailment was the toll it took on her worship. According to the law, Veronica was perpetually unclean. Every person she came in contact with, the clothes she wore, the very bed she slept in, were considered unclean. She was excluded from the temple or synagogue. She was a marked pariah to all who knew her.

The day the Healer passed, she felt an unceasing unction to reach Him. She had heard the miraculous tales. Covering her entire body, she rushed into a crowd that had surrounded Him. "If I only touch the edge of his cloak, I will be healed." And when she did touch Him, He stopped and recognized her among the throng of people. "Daughter, your faith has healed you. Go in peace." Those words would forever resonate in her heart.

The time was now! Pushing through the crowds once again, she miraculously made it past the soldiers and thrust a cool, wet cloth tenderly on His face. For a moment, He felt sweet relief from the heat and pain. His eyes were cleared of the blinding blood.

The soldiers were upon her swiftly, throwing her back into the crowd. There she stood watching. He gazed at her and smiled. As He continued toward Golgotha, she clutched the bloody rag to her breast and whispered, "I am again healed."

Lord Jesus Christ, have mercy upon me.

Daily I press through to You, Lord.
I press through the mediocrity that drowns me,
the pain of sin, the deafening circumstances,
and the overflowing schedules that doggedly overwhelm me.
I press toward You, just to touch the hem of Your robe.
I have to give back to You.
I do not care if my hands are bloodied.
I thrust through the crowd only to reach You.
My love for You overcomes any fears that whisper in my ears.
You said that if I give to the least of these, I give to You.
Today, my God, show me the least,
that I may serve them and touch You.
I will take a risk of love and spread compassion,
even if it soils my hands.
Amidst those in pain and ugliness,
the rejected and the suffering,
I will find You and I will take the cool cloth
of compassion and love to relieve their suffering.
In doing so, I will put that cool cloth upon Your brow
and demonstrate my love for You.

Lord Jesus Christ, have mercy upon me.

Even though I walk
through the valley of the
shadow of death,
I will fear no evil,
for you are with me;
your rod and your staff,
they comfort me.

Psalm 23:4

Second Fall

Stand firm like an anvil under the hammer. It is like a great athlete to take the blows and yet win the fight.
Ignatius to Polycarp, First Century

He then began to teach them that the Son of Man must suffer many things and be rejected by the elders, chief priests and teachers of the law, and that he must be killed and after three days rise again. Then he called the crowd to him along with his disciples and said: "If anyone would come after me, he must deny himself and take up his cross and follow me. For whoever wants to save his life will lose it, but whoever loses his life for me and for the gospel will save it."
Mark 8:31, 34–35

Thank you for allowing me a bit of rest before continuing my strange account. I want to remind you that I clearly understand the ramifications of resigning my post as a centurion. It will most certainly bring dishonor to my family. But the disgrace I have already been a part of makes any other dishonor seem trite.

I believe I left off my story with the one they called the King of the Jews being inhumanely beaten by my men. From there, he was led on the streets through the city. The crowds gathered as always, but this time en masse, so our progress was slow. At one point, the prisoner became so weakened that I seized a bystander to take the crossbeam from him.

When we came to the hill of Ghareb, the law prescribed that those being executed must, if possible, bear their burden of execution. This one who was beaten beyond recognition stopped. On his own volition, he took the beam from the bystander and whispered something into his ear.

I was stunned. Never in all my years as an officer in the Roman army have I witnessed such fortitude and determination.

Slowly, he began to work his way up the hill. I held the soldiers back from any abuse simply to watch what he would do next. I looked at his eyes, and they were set as firmly as the giant Gibraltar that sits at the gates of the Great Sea.

Half way up his ascent, he lost his footing. The small jagged rocks that lay upon the entire path were cutting into His unprotected feet. Stumbling, he fell again with a nasty thud. I thought he was finally spent. But to my sheer amazement, he pushed up from the dust and stood once again. Grabbing the beam, he again continued his climb. What was this man's mission? Why did he persevere toward his death with such passion?

I had joined the army, following in the footsteps of my father and his father before him. They were the bravest of men and willing to lay their lives down for the Empire. They had something beyond mere belief. They had conviction. I have come to realize that beliefs are something you argue about. Conviction is something you will die for.

A person with no convictions is at the mercy of circumstance. This man had a conviction and resilience stronger than any I have ever witnessed. I will go so far as to say that he seemed in control of his own execution. I was humbled by his sheer tenacity.

Yet, the strangest part of this tale is still to be told.

Lord Jesus Christ, have mercy upon me.

I believe in God, the Father Almighty,
Maker of heaven and earth;
And in Jesus Christ His only Son our Lord;
who was conceived by the Holy Spirit,
born of the Virgin Mary,
suffered under Pontius Pilate,
was crucified, dead, and buried.
He descended into hell.
The third day, He rose again from the dead.
He ascended into heaven and
sits at the right hand of God the Father Almighty,
from where He shall come to judge the quick and the dead.
I believe in the Holy Spirit,
the holy Catholic church, the communion of saints,
the forgiveness of sins, the resurrection of the body,
and the life everlasting. Amen.

I believe these things, Lord.
Help me to live them, moving beyond belief into conviction.

Lord Jesus Christ, have mercy upon me.

The high places of
wickedness
will be destroyed—it is the
sin of Israel.
Thorns and thistles will
grow up and cover their altars
Then they will say to the
mountains, "Cover us!"
and to the hills, "Fall on us!"

Hosea 10:8

The Weeping

Where words are scarce, they are seldom spent in vain,
For they breathe truth that breathe their words in pain.
William Shakespeare, *Richard II*

A large number of people followed him, including women who mourned and wailed for him. Jesus turned and said to them, "Daughters of Jerusalem, do not weep for me; weep for yourselves and for your children. For the time will come when you will say, 'Blessed are the barren women, the wombs that never bore and the breasts that never nursed!' Then 'they will say to the mountains, "Fall on us!" and to the hills, "Cover us!"' For if men do these things when the tree is green, what will happen when it is dry?"
Luke 23:27–31

The day He had visited the home of Jarius, the ruler of the synagogue, Jesus had run into this same crowd, and it was not a pleasant experience. He had, in fact, firmly rebuked them. "Why make this commotion and weep? The child is not dead, but sleeping." Their pitiful sobs and horrendous wailing for the dead stopped instantly, replaced by raucous laughter and mean-spirited ridicule. The only thing that caused their amusement to cease was the little girl emerging from her home, very much alive.

These women had an odd place in Jewish culture. They were official wailers who wept for the highest bidder. The amount of love and honor for the deceased was proven by the number of mourners hired to wail for the dead. This practice was a hypocrisy that was sadly accepted as normal and correct. Yet, paying for mourning never healed a single heart.

Now, once again, as He topped the hill of Golgotha, Jesus heard the shrill pitch of their howling voices. This was their charity—their work of mercy. They would give a dramatic performance for the condemned on this holy day eve. Who knows? Maybe it would open up more business for them in the future. But the Savior would not be mocked.

Stopping directly in front of the small cluster of women, He spoke. "Daughters of Jerusalem, do not weep for me; weep for yourselves and for your children. For the time will come when you will say, 'Blessed are the barren women, the wombs that never bore and the breasts that never nursed!' Then 'they will say to the mountains, "Fall on us!" and to the hills, "Cover us!"'"

They were stunned into silence. He wanted their eyes opened to the greater drama unfolding around them. Words of truth rang in the ears of the crowd. Weep against evil, for agony does not entomb Me! Do not allow your tears to blind you from the truth that stands in front of you. You are broken people who would rather hide behind tears than deal with the truth.

As the Christ continued toward His place of execution, the women stood still. They were too curious to leave and too afraid to wail. Soon after, their insincere tears were replaced by genuine grief. One by one they departed, contemplating their futures and the future of Jerusalem. And not an eye was dry.

Lord Jesus Christ, have mercy upon me.

May I cry only genuine tears of repentance
and not take advantage of Your mercy, Lord.
I do not want to feel sorry for myself,
so help me cry for the wounded and lost.
Let me to weep because of evil,
and allow that weeping to lead to action.
Always let my tears be as liquid pearl,
an offering of worth before Your throne.

Lord Jesus Christ, have mercy upon me.

Many bulls surround me;
strong bulls of Bashan
encircle me.
Roaring lions tearing
their prey open their
mouths wide against me.

Psalm 22:12-13

To get rid of an enemy, one must love him.
Leo Tolstoy

The teachers of the law and the Pharisees brought in a woman caught in adultery. They made her stand before the group and said to Jesus, "Teacher, this woman was caught in the act of adultery. In the Law Moses commanded us to stone such women. Now what do you say?" They were using this question as a trap, in order to have a basis for accusing him. But Jesus bent down and started to write on the ground with his finger. When they kept on questioning him, he straightened up and said to them, "If any one of you is without sin, let him be the first to throw a stone at her." Again he stooped down and wrote on the ground. At this, those who heard began to go away one at a time, the older ones first, until only Jesus was left, with the woman still standing there. Jesus straightened up and asked her, "Woman, where are they?"
John 8:3–10

Cresting the hill of Golgotha, the One called Jesus of Nazareth became breathless. His footing was erratic but His pace steady. It took all of His concentration to get one foot in front of the other. The soldiers imagined that they were keeping Him moving, but it was sheer will and prayer that kept the Lamb of God on His path.

Atop the end of His journey, a fair-sized crowd had amassed. Its anger rumbled in His ears. The soldiers held the crowd's physical presence at bay but they could not contain the throng's hatred of Him. Some threw stones at His beaten body. Most of the people just screamed epithets of hatred. His accusers were many: soldiers, Sanhedrin, common folk, and devils galore.

During His last few footsteps, He once again felt the agony of His body and blacked out for a brief second. His legs failed as He crumpled to the ground like a newborn calf. As blood rushed from His head, the voices became muted. He could still hear laughing.

Angel and devil alike wondered what compelled the Son of God forward. His followers had denied Him and He was ridiculed by the religious leaders. Soldiers who hated anything Jewish had beaten Him ferociously, and now on top of all that, they laughed.

All seemed to be casting stones and no one came to His aid as He lay in the dirt. His hands had always brought healing, tenderness, and love. Now, when He needed a hand in return, none could be found. The only thing that met Him was mockery and the lash.

So why did He continue toward Golgotha? Love. This was a love that emanated far outside of human understanding. This love was His being. It was all that had ever motivated Him, and now was no different. He treasured these people and saw through their shells of insecurity, prejudice, bitterness, and blame. Eternal eyes broke through the masks, realizing who these individuals were: God's children. He also knew that many of those who gathered today would one day be drawn to His throne. He had no room in His heart for hatred, no room for enemies.

Four large hands gripped Him by His shoulders, pulling Him into a standing position. He would continue, for the end was soon at hand.

Lord Jesus Christ, have mercy upon me.

God, grant me the patience to reach those
who are intolerant, cruel, envious, and braggarts.
Teach me to pray for those who are proud, rude,
and out for only themselves.
Give me the grace to unconditionally love
those who are angry and bitter.
I want to demonstrate truth
to those enmeshed in evil
through trust in Your Word,
hope in Your Son,
and perseverance in the Holy Spirit.
And Father, if I am any of those things I just mentioned,
deal with my heart so I may never turn aside from
Your gracious gift of love.

Lord Jesus Christ, have mercy upon me.

Carrying
his **own cross**,
he went **out** to the place of
the Skull
(which in Aramaic is called Golgotha).

John 19:17

Golgotha

Death is a debt which must at all events be paid.
Justin, martyr

The high priest carries the blood of animals into the Most Holy Place as a sin offering, but the bodies are burned outside the camp. And so Jesus also suffered outside the city gate to make the people holy through his own blood.

Hebrews 13:11–12

And He, bearing His cross, went out to a place called the Place of a Skull, which is called in Hebrew, Golgotha.
John 19:17 (NKJV)

Born in the Garden of Eden, it was mankind's greatest enemy. Adam—its liberator—had unleashed this beast that would devastate the cosmos. Its insatiable appetite demanded the ultimate price from every living creature. This monstrosity, Death, had become more powerful than the Prince of the Air. In fact, Death deemed itself to be more powerful than the Almighty.

Every human on this miserable, dusty sphere was its timid subject. From the moment these souls emerged from their mothers' wombs, they started the inevitable journey toward mortality. Of course, there had been a few occasions when the Creator had postponed the unavoidable, but in the end, all living things met Death. And they were dreadfully afraid; almost every one of them trembled at the thought of their final appointment. That is, until Jesus came along.

This One that called Himself the Son of God was never afraid. Throughout His entire life, they had confronted one another. In fact, Death had attempted, in vain, to exterminate this One who had such a completely different origin than all the other despondent humans on the planet.

Death's desperation had grown to heights it never realized possible. And that despair was stimulated by something it had only experienced through its encounters with Him. Death had learned to fear. This Son had snatched back some of those whom Death had firmly in its control. Victory was ripped from its claws every time the Son revived Death's victims from the grave.

Who or what was this Man? This thought caused a shiver to run down its cold spine. Could this One be a God-Man? If He was a God-Man, could He die?

Death became consumed with causing the Son's end. And this is where it would happen. The place where the Son had carried His cross was known as Golgotha to the Hebrews; Calvaria to the Romans. The name intoned the same fate. This was Death's terrain. The barren, stony knoll that sat just outside of Jerusalem's gates loosely resembled a skull. Because it was considered a foreboding place to the Jews, the Romans took advantage of their superstitions and selected it as a place of execution. Sitting on a well-traveled road into the city, this hill served as a chilling reminder of Roman rule.

Death stood atop the hill, watching its victim slowly climb the last ridge. The Son would not escape again. Death would murder Life!

Lord Jesus Christ, have mercy upon me.

Death entered through one man's disobedience,
and was banished through one Man's obedience.
Oh Christ, Son of God, You have indeed
been raised from the dead.
You have vanquished our greatest enemy, death,
and in turn given us resurrection.
Let us always remember that
death has been swallowed up in victory.
Where, O death, is your victory?
Where, O death, is your sting?
For we have the victory through Christ Jesus our Lord.

Lord Jesus Christ, have mercy upon me.

There they offered Jesus wine to drink, mixed with gall [and myrrh]; but after tasting it, he refused to drink it.

Matthew 27:34

Myrrh and Gall

The leg does not feel the fetter when the spirit is in heaven.
Tertullian, "To the Martyrs"

You know how I am scorned, disgraced and shamed;
all my enemies are before you.
Scorn has broken my heart and has left me helpless;
I looked for sympathy, but there was none,
for comforters, but I found none.
They put gall in my food and gave me vinegar for my thirst.
Psalm 69:19–21

They came to the place called Golgotha. . . . Two other men, both criminals, were also led out to be executed.
Matthew 27:33 and Luke 23:32

"**I** will never forget those eyes. His gaze made me feel as if I looked into the face of God. Forgive me, for I do not wish to be blasphemous, but it makes me think the rumors are true. This Man was a prophet." The meek woman spoke in hushed tones to her family during the Passover meal. Obviously shaken, her family moved closer around her. They were captivated by the tale of her encounter with the crucified Rabbi from Galilee.

She had a calling that was very unique. Most thought her somewhat mad for performing her acts of mercy. She saw herself simply as an instrument of God's great compassion. On execution days, this woman, along with a few others, stationed herself at the top of Golgotha. As the doomed prisoners crested the fated hill, these women would administer a guarded medicine to the condemned.

The solution was a careful mixture of vinegar wine, gall, and myrrh. The wine was symbolic of the blood of sacrifice. It was to be hoped that the criminal facing imminent death would make his peace before entering Sheol. The gall came from a poisonous herb. Not only did it dull the senses—making the terrible pain of crucifixion easier to bear—but it also reminded the prisoners of the bitterness of sin that brought them to this point. Because of the sour bite of the gall, sweet-smelling and anesthetic myrrh was added to balance out the taste. Myrrh was commonly used in burial. So in a way, the liquid was dispensed to the prisoners to prepare them for death.

Three were sentenced to death on this holy day eve. The first criminal, a common crook, drank with a ravenous thirst. Fear filled his eyes. The second thief was a man consumed with a bitter rage. He took a deep draught of the liquid, then cursed the hands that gave it to him. But as the Rabbi came forward, something happened that this worker of mercy had never observed before. He took a small sip of the medicine and immediately stopped.

"He looked up at me. His face was marred beyond that of any criminal I have ever relieved. Blood covered His brow. He smiled at me. I was not prepared for His sentiment. He shook his head slightly as if to say, 'No thank you dear woman.' Those lovely, kind eyes looked deep into me and I felt like I could hear His voice in my head saying, 'I must face My suffering with complete control of My mind. When I encounter death, I will not be numbed.' As those three walked toward death, I knew I would never forget the gall of fear and bitterness in the two thieves and the myrrh of faith in the Rabbi."

Lord Jesus Christ, have mercy upon me.

In my life, I cannot control circumstance.
Neither can I control the decisions of others that affect me.
What I can choose is how I allow
those things to affect and change me.
Keep my mind and my heart from the bitter gall
that could corrupt every fraction of my life.
Instead, fill me with the sweet aroma of the Holy Spirit
who works in all things for the good of those
who have been called according to His purpose.

Lord Jesus Christ, have mercy upon me.

They divide **my** garments
among them and
cast lots
for **my clothing.**

Psalm 22:18

Stripped

> A mountain tree if it would see
> The far horizons and the stars,
> May never know a sheltered place
> Nor grow symmetrical in grace.
> Such trees must battle doggedly
> The blasts, and bear the scars.
> **Loyal Marion Thompson, "Mountain Tree"**

They [the soldiers] took his clothes, dividing them into four shares, one for each of them, with the undergarment remaining. This garment was seamless, woven in one piece from top to bottom. "Let's not tear it," they said to one another. "Let's decide by lot who will get it." This happened that the scripture might be fulfilled which said, "They divided my garments among them and cast lots for my clothing." So this is what the soldiers did. And sitting down, they kept watch over him there.

John 19:23–24 and Matthew 27:36

The deed was done. Adam's surrender to serpentine deception had caused a detonation of death that traveled outward from the garden, laying waste to the entire cosmos. For the first time, man felt the brutal weight of shame. Purity was stripped away.

The Lord walked through the garden calling for His children saying, "Where are you?" Adam answered in hushed disgrace, "I heard You in the garden, and I was afraid because I was naked; so I hid."

The Lord Himself sacrificed an animal to make garments for His children, covering the loss of innocence and glory.

As Christ reached the site of execution, the guards removed the crossbeam from His neck. Standing motionless, the temporary reprieve of weight seemed wondrous. Activity continued around Him. The two men before Him screamed as they were nailed to the beams.

Jesus waited. Two soldiers approached Him and removed His belt, head covering, and outer robe. Noticing the fine quality of His inner garment, they took precautions in stripping it off His body. To these hardened men, the prisoner's bloodied, seamless tunic was much more valuable than His life. As they stripped it from His upper body, coagulated wounds that had drawn to the cloth were ripped open. Again, blood flowed.

But one final act of humiliation would occur. In customary cruelty, they stripped Him of His loincloth, leaving only shame and humiliation. In a few moments, the execution squad would roll dice for His garments directly below His torn body. The Christ would be displayed, utterly exposed before all who mocked, wept, and worshipped.

The deed was done. Christ's obedience to God would cause a chain reaction of life and forgiveness that would travel outward from Golgotha toward the whole of creation. Through the stripping, the Son would replace the weight of the crossbeam with the weight of mankind's shame. The Father would soon turn away from the Son. He knew His Son must pay the grave debt of mankind alone. His death would bring the garment of incorruptibility and glory back to mankind.

Lord Jesus Christ, have mercy upon me.

Many times, Lord, I attempt to cover my shame
with something on the outside.
I wear masks that hide my true feelings.
I put on clothes, hoping they will cause others to accept me.
I buy material possessions as an attempt
to fill an empty spot in my life.
I become what I believe others want me to be
so that I will not feel alone.
But deep inside, I still feel isolated
and cut off from true life.
Help me to replace my masks with
the courage to be honest with my emotions.
Give me the understanding
that it is not what I wear on the outside,
but who I am on the inside that brings worth to my life.
I do not want possessions to fill the empty places in my heart,
because they never do.
Give me a greater understanding of my purpose
and allow that to fill my time.
Help me to be only what You have created me to be,
and realize that You never leave me nor forsake me.
Without Your death I would remain naked and alone,
cut off from Your presence and my purpose.
I, once again, remember that You cover me.

Lord Jesus Christ, have mercy upon me.

Dogs have surrounded me;
a band of evil men
has encircled me,
they have pierced
my hands and my feet.

Psalm 22:16

Crucified

One hour of unquestioning surrender to God's will is of greater value
than all feelings of devotion and consolation.

Mother Teresa

It was the third hour when they crucified him. Two robbers were
crucified with him, one on his right and one on his left. Those who
passed by hurled insults at him, shaking their heads and saying, "You
who are going to destroy the temple and build it in three days, save
yourself! Come down from the cross, if you are the Son of God!" Jesus
said, "Father, forgive them, for they do not know what they are doing."
. . . The people stood watching, and the rulers even sneered at him.
They said, "He saved others; let him save himself if he is the Christ of
God, the Chosen One."

Mark 15:25; Matthew 27:38–40; and Luke 23:34–35

As the Son of God was stripped, the execution squad nailed crossbeam to post. It was just after nine o'clock, and they were already weary of the morning's activities. Before they could seize their prisoner, He moved toward the wood as if an invisible force compelled Him forward.

He offered no resistance when they stretched His arm upon the beam. Lying face up, the first spike was carefully placed between the bones in His wrist. The hammer fell in rapid strokes, severing skin, muscle, and bone. The echo of metal and the vibration of wood could not drown out His scream, which seemed to overshadow the whole of Jerusalem. His cry intermingled with the cries of hundreds of lambs being led to the slaughter. How many blows would it take?

Without a moment of mercy, the soldiers grabbed His other arm and pulled, separating the shoulders with a wicked snap. Spikes pierced the One who cured lepers, wiped away blindness, and lovingly held children. Torn flesh and burst arteries almost caused Him to go unconscious as the Carpenter was once again joined to wood.

Placing His legs on the post, they purposefully aimed the nail through the bones in the center of His feet. This would securely hold the lower body in a sitting position. All three nails had been placed through major nerves in the limbs. The victim could not move without sending razor-sharp pains that traveled through the length of the body.

Once Jesus was attached to the tree, the soldiers lifted Him into place. As the bottom of the cross slipped into the ground supports, it quickly slid into place, jarring His body with the full impact of the drop. In His momentary delirium of pain, He heard a taunting voice in the crowd that quickly gathered around the setting of His torture.

"You who will destroy the temple and build it in three days, save yourself! Come down from the cross, if you are the Son of God!" His naysayers snickered at the venomous comment. Knowing His fate was sealed, they hushed, waiting to hear a rebuttal of some kind.

Instead, He whispered a statement that caused the soldiers to stare, His followers to weep, and His accusers to rile in an outburst of fury. "Father, forgive them, for they do not know what they are doing." Something other than nails was holding Him to this cross.

Lord Jesus Christ, have mercy upon me.

I have been crucified with Christ
Which means I no longer live.
Yet, Christ lives within me!

The life I live in this body,
I live by faith and trust in the Son of God
Who loved me
And gave Himself for me.
Becoming obedient unto death;
Even death upon a cross.

Lord Jesus Christ, have mercy upon me.

Rejoice greatly,
O Daughter of Zion!
Shout, Daughter of
Jerusalem!
See, your king comes to you,
righteous and having
salvation.

Zechariah 9:9

Sign

The silence is never broken except to shout the truth.
Flannery O'Connor, *The Violent Bear It Away*

Pilate had a notice prepared and fastened to the cross. It read: JESUS OF NAZARETH, THE KING OF THE JEWS. Many of the Jews read this sign, for the place where Jesus was crucified was near the city, and the sign was written in Aramaic, Latin and Greek. The chief priests of the Jews protested to Pilate, "Do not write 'The King of the Jews,' but that this man claimed to be king of the Jews." Pilate answered, "What I have written, I have written."

John 19:19–22

"Excuse me, Prefect. They are back again to take audience with you." The soldier had a reason to be sheepish with his announcement. The early morning trial had set Pilate in a foul mood. "Show them in!" This had been the strangest of days. Pilate reasoned that he had done enough dirty work for these men, and he hoped his little joke was the incentive that compelled them to return so soon.

Several principal priests of Jerusalem marched into the Roman courtyard with scowls on their brows; their robes ripped in protest. "What is the meaning of this outrage! Why do you disgrace us in this manner?"

Pilate smiled for the first time this day. His final message to these bothersome religious zealots had worked beautifully. Roman custom demanded that every man condemned to the cross have their name and crimes posted on a titulus for all to witness. This sign was positioned as a warning. Pilate, feeling humiliated by the trap these men had set for him, decided to disgrace them publicly in return. The sign he would post over their hated foe would read: JESUS OF NAZARETH, THE KING OF THE JEWS. To rub salt into the wound, Pilate would write it in Aramaic, Latin, and Greek. All would grasp why this man was crucified.

Growling like cornered beasts, the leaders fired their demands. "Do not write 'THE KING OF THE JEWS,' but that this man claimed to be king of the Jews."

Pilate loosed a chortle that tinged on madness. Then he suddenly took a deadly tone. "What I have written, I have written."

Turning around, he left the courtyard without another glance toward his unwanted visitors. This sign would act as his personal slur to the Jewish aspirations of independence. The game would continue, but he would no longer be a player. Pilate, representative of the Roman government and the Gentile world, had completed his role by signing the death warrant. The memory of his signature remained in the forefront of his mind, and convinced him that the sign would stay.

Being the King of the Jews was Jesus' only crime. He would be condemned by Jew and Gentile; rich and poor; religious and pagan alike. And the sign over His beaten brow would read: JESUS OF NAZARETH, THE KING OF THE JEWS.

Lord Jesus Christ, have mercy upon me.

I am on the journey constantly looking for a sign of
which way to turn—where to go.
You said, Lord Christ, that You only go
where the Father leads.
I have committed to follow You, Jesus.
Take me where the Father wills as I daily follow You.
And let me comprehend the sign they posted over You:
Jesus of Nazareth—King of the Jews.

Lord Jesus Christ, have mercy upon me.

Therefore
    I will give him a portion
among the **great**, and he **will**
    divide the **spoils** with the **strong**,
because he poured out **his life**
    unto death, and was numbered
with the **transgressors**.
    For he bore the sin of many, and
made intercession for the
    transgressors.

Isaiah 53:12

Two Thieves

> *Two men look out through the same bars:*
> *One sees the mud, and one the stars.*
> **Frederick Langbridge**

Two robbers were crucified with him, one on his right and one on his left. In the same way the chief priests, the teachers of the law and the elders mocked him. "He saved others," they said, "but he can't save himself! He's the King of Israel! Let him come down now from the cross, and we will believe in him. He trusts in God. Let God rescue him now if he wants him, for he said, 'I am the Son of God.'" In the same way the robbers who were crucified with him also heaped insults on him.

Matthew 27:38, 41–44

One of the criminals who hung there hurled insults at him: "Aren't you the Christ? Save yourself and us!" But the other criminal rebuked him. "Don't you fear God," he said, "since you are under the same sentence? We are punished justly, for we are getting what our deeds deserve. But this man has done nothing wrong." Then he said, "Jesus, remember me when you come into your kingdom." Jesus answered him, "I tell you the truth, today you will be with me in paradise."

Luke 23:39–43

I already feel Sheol's breath on my neck, and there is no escape. I am so afraid . . . so very afraid. I cry out to You, Lord.

I have run from You since I left my family in pursuit of fortune. Oh, how I wounded them with my departure. Do they know what has become of me? Do they realize that I have become a vile worm living off the handouts of others and stealing whenever I was able?

This is the death I have deserved. But I am not prepared to go to the grave. Would You forgive this worm, Lord? Or is this a just punishment for a prodigal son of Israel?

Forgive me for mocking the Rabbi that hangs next to me. I have heard of His works. Even now I see forgiveness and love in His eyes. To look into them is to realize the sin that has overtaken my heart. Lord, help Him. Lord, forgive me . . .

The crowd was growing around the Nazarene. A few of His closest companions, including His mother, had defied the mockery of the mob to be with Him in His last few moments of life. But the angered priests and teachers derided Him with a renewed fervor.

Relieved that the crowd was ignoring them, the two thieves who were being crucified with Him had joined in the ridicule. But the one on His right, the one that seemed so afraid, started to cry. Closing his eyes, he began to pray quietly.

The thief on the left, to the joy of the mob, screamed at the Man in the middle. "Aren't you the Christ? Save yourself and us!"

The crucified thief on the right of the Nazarene immediately opened his eyes. His fear was now replaced with a courage previously unknown to him. "Don't you fear God," he said with a formidable voice, "since you are under the same sentence? We are punished justly, for we are receiving what our deeds deserve. But this man has done nothing wrong."

Turning to the One whose eyes had softened his hardened and fearful heart, he said, "Jesus, remember me when you come into your kingdom."

Jesus answered him, "I tell you the truth, today you will be with Me in paradise."

Thank You, Lord. Today I have seen the Son. Tonight the Father will embrace me. I am again a child of Israel . . .

Lord Jesus Christ, have mercy upon me.

There are always choices before me.
Choices that lead toward righteousness
and those that take me down a road of destruction.
How often have I played the prodigal child?
So many times I have chosen what I knew to be sin.
Oh, what a wretched man I am.
But when I gaze into Your eyes,
my hardened heart softens.
When I stop and look at Your face,
I reject the path of sin and self.
Father, I do not ever want to lose sight of Your eyes.
I want to see You face to face every day.
Keep me on the path to Your kingdom
so I may one day hear You say,
"Well done my good and faithful servant."

Lord Jesus Christ, have mercy upon me.

Therefore
the **Lord** himself
will **give you** a sign:
The **virgin** will be with child
and will **give birth** to a
son, and will call him
Immanuel.

Isaiah 7:14

Caregiver

Gentleness is captivating! Gentleness in a person's eyes, in the tone of his voice. Nothing resists the power of supernatural and persevering serenity. It is the drop of water which seeps through the hardest rock.

Mother Teresa

Near the cross of Jesus stood his mother, his mother's sister, Mary the wife of Clopas, and Mary Magdalene. When Jesus saw his mother there, and the disciple whom he loved standing nearby, he said to his mother, "Dear woman, here is your son," and to the disciple, "Here is your mother." From that time on, this disciple took her into his home.

John 19:25–27

"**O**ld man. Hey, son of Zebedee . . . are you awake?"

"Yes, Tychicus. I have not slumbered as of yet." John was always ready during the evening hours, for this was the time of storytelling.

Ever since he had landed upon this desolate and barren rock known as the Isle of Patmos, he had become a favorite among the other convicts. They were well aware of the rumor about John's submersion into a vat of boiling oil by the enraged emperor, and how it had not injured him. What startled them was his old age. Apparently, if the emperor could not torture John, he would make the last few years of his life miserable with the sentence of hard labor.

To them, John was an inspiration. What they loved more than anything else were his late-night tales of the miracle worker of Palestine.

"Now, where did I leave off last night?" spoke John in a thoughtful tone.

"This One you serve, your God the Christ, was on the cross," said Tychicus.

"Oh, yes. Now I remember. Do you wish me to continue?"

Another prisoner waiting for the tale spoke. "Now we know why He called you the Son of Thunder. You always like to stir us up for your tales. Please begin."

"Yes, yes. You are right. I must continue. As I was saying yester eve, a few women and I were standing at the foot of His cross, along with soldiers and a vast crowd that railed against Him. His mother, Mary, was crying in anguish. I wrapped my arms around her slender frame. To see her son in so much pain was more than she could bear.

"I distinctly remember Jesus looking down at us. His face, horribly marred, could not hide His compassion for His mother. His eyes of love were a stark contrast compared to the cruelty and indifference that encircled Him. He spoke to her tenderly. 'Dear woman, here is your son.'

"Turning to me, He charged me to keep her safe. She was to be as my very mother. In the moment of His utmost suffering, He took time to care for her future. As the eldest son, He was responsible for Mary. The Son who was once cradled in her arms would always be her caregiver."

Their contemplative silence spoke more than any words they could have mustered. Finally, Tychicus whispered what all the other men were thinking. "Please finish, John, and do not stop until we know what happened to your Holy One, Jesus."

John smiled. The story, as always, would continue.

Lord Jesus Christ, have mercy upon me.

Even on the cross, You cared for your mother
who had so often cared for You.
Father, I want to thank you for my parents.
For what I learned from them, and how they loved me.
God, I ask You to bless and keep safe those
who have been spiritual parents in my life.
Through the truth, love, and transparency of their lives,
I have been drawn to You.
And for those times when my parents were,
for whatever reason, not near,
I praise You for being my loving Father.
You have never left nor forsaken me.

Lord Jesus Christ, have mercy upon me.

It was now about the
sixth hour, and
darkness came over
the **whole land**
until the **ninth** hour,
for the sun **stopped**
shining.

Luke 23:44-45

Darkness

No light, but rather darkness visible.
John Milton, *Paradise Lost*

Then the LORD said to Moses, "Stretch out your hand toward the sky so that darkness will spread over Egypt—darkness that can be felt." So Moses stretched out his hand toward the sky, and total darkness covered all Egypt for three days. Yet all the Israelites had light in the places where they lived.

Exodus 10:21–23

The sun's light failed, so that darkness came over the whole land until the ninth hour.

Luke 23:44 (NJB)

At noon the darkness descended, consuming all light. Around the world many began to wonder if they would ever see sunrise again. What the witnesses of the crucifixion could not see was the gathering that caused the darkness. Sin, upon entering the human race through Adam, became an unquenchable beast that ruptured the fabric of creation.

Man had forever scratched at the wound of sin that was now embedded in his psyche. He would scrape it until it bled, but relief was never found. This wound then lead to torment and eventually death. Mankind had become a zoo of lusts and inaccessible ambitions. Fear, mistrust, hatred, and intolerance invigorated man's insatiable desire for power, and the natural outcome was wars of domination. Mankind wallowed in the vomit of its own corruption, and fought for the right to do so. The dungeon of self was securely sealed, and none could escape. Only shadows of hope remained.

A bounty of righteousness was demanded. And the very Judge that set the bounty had sent His Son to pay the price in full. He was the Lamb of God, slain from the foundation of creation. This was the only way mankind would ever be what it was designed to become. Hanging on the cross and experiencing extreme physical torture was a meager precursor to the event now unfolding in the hidden regions that sat outside creation and the heavens.

Across creation and time itself, the entirety of sin gathered. Every transgression, crime, and wrongdoing ever committed, or to be committed, drew together as an invisible cloud around the cross. The imperceptible accumulation of this colossal contagion was so potent that it caused the blotting out of the sun. Slowly building up momentum, the gathering tempest whirled around the Son. For three hours, this invisible cyclone escalated until it completely enveloped Him.

In a jarring moment, the tempest exploded upward as one massive leviathan. The angels almost sighed in relief, believing this to be the end of the battle. But the entity, now hovering out of sight above the Son, shot back down like a deadly missile. As it reached the Christ, it entered into Him with a deafening roar. This monster of iniquity penetrated wholly into the sinless One, filling Him with the poison of mankind, and making Him sin.

Lord Jesus Christ, have mercy upon me.

My sin is ever before my eyes.
And it is these sins, known and unknown,
that compelled You to the cross.
I pause now and take this time of solemn confession
to acknowledge my sin as I freely confess it before You.
I thank You, Lord, that You have declared Yourself
faithful and just to forgive me of my sins
if I confess them to You.
Help me to go and sin no more.
Hide Your face from my sins and blot out all my iniquity.
Create in me a pure heart, O God,
and renew a steadfast spirit within me.
Do not cast me from Your presence
nor take Your Holy Spirit from me.
Restore to me the joy of Your salvation
and grant me a willing spirit to sustain me.

Lord Jesus Christ, have mercy upon me.

My God, my God,
why have you **forsaken** me?
Why are you **so** far
from **saving** me,
so **far** from the **words**
of my **groaning**?

Psalm 22:1

Forsaken

"As our lives unfold, at first we yawn, but later the yawn turns into a scream."

Søren Kierkegaard

*They put gall in my food
and gave me vinegar for my thirst.*
Psalm 69:21

About the ninth hour Jesus cried out in a loud voice, "Eloi, Eloi, lama sabachthani?"—which means, "My God, my God, why have you forsaken me?" When some of those standing there heard this, they said, "He's calling Elijah." Later, knowing that all was now completed, and so the Scripture would be fulfilled, Jesus said, "I am thirsty." A jar of wine vinegar was there. Immediately one of them ran and got a sponge. He filled it with wine vinegar, put it on a [stalk of the hyssop plant], and offered it to Jesus to drink. The rest said, "Now leave him alone. Let's see if Elijah comes to save him."
Matthew 27:46–49 and John 19:28–29

The tortures, rejection, and pain of frail humanity had come to a crescendo on the hill of Golgotha. The Son hung upon the tree. And now, for the first time, He could not sense the Father's presence.

Incarnation had always been in fellowship with Father and Spirit. Separation was unknown in the Godhead. But the One slain before the foundations of the world had become sin. He was not a representative of sin as the sacrificial lambs in the temple. He had become the embodiment of sin. His sacrifice would once and for all times pay the bond price for man's rebellion toward God. This fact did not ease the horrifying sorrow of the moment. This was the instant He had cried out about in Gethsemane. "Father, if it is Your will let this cup pass . . ." The cup had not passed, and He would drink deep of its bitter waters. The Son of God would now know what it meant to be forsaken and alone.

In a throaty and parched voice, He verbalized His inward battle: "My God, my God, why have you forsaken me . . ." The naysayers at His feet continued to mock the One that was paying the price for their sins, even for the very mockery in which they were now engaged. One young man began to call out to the crowd. "Look, he calls for Elijah to help him! 'Elijah, Elijah. Where are you? Your faithful servant is calling.'" The scorn and sarcasm in his voice had taken on a sinister tone.

"I am thirsty," Jesus said, looking at a Roman soldier holding the crowd back at the foot of the cross. The soldier took a dirty sponge and soaked it in the bucket of wine vinegar and water that sat nearby. Taking a hyssop stalk, he lifted the sponge to the lips of Jesus. The crowd railed at the soldier for his moment of mercy. How ironic that the One who opened up wells of living water would Himself thirst.

As Jesus sipped on the sponge, He noticed the hyssop branch. He recalled a dark night over a thousand years earlier. Jewish families were huddled in their homes by firelight. They were partaking of the Passover lamb and preparing for a long journey. Throughout Egypt they could hear the wailing of families who were losing their firstborn to the angel of death. The only thing that had kept their families safe was the blood of the lamb painted over the doorposts of their homes with the branch of the hyssop.

The Christ came back to Himself. He knew it was finished.

Lord Jesus Christ, have mercy upon me.

Because Christ was beaten
I can be healed.

Because Christ was forsaken
I am unconditionally accepted.

Because Christ died
I will remain alive.

Lord Jesus Christ, have mercy upon me.

Into your hands
I commit my spirit;
redeem me, O LORD,
the God of truth.

Psalm 31:5

Finished

For tho' from out our bourne of Time and Place
The flood may bear me far,
I hope to see my Pilot face to face
When I have crost the bar.
Alfred, Lord Tennyson, "Crossing the Bar"

When he had received the drink, Jesus said, "It is finished." Jesus called out with a loud voice, "Father, into your hands I commit my spirit." With that, he bowed his head and gave up his spirit.
Luke 23:46 and John 19:30

Death had waited and watched the Son. Several times, over the last few hours, it had attempted to snuff out His life. Confused, this creature of destruction simply stared with an odd mix of curiosity and revulsion.

Of all the cruel tortures man had devised, crucifixion was Death's favorite. The Romans brought a person to the brink of eternity and held them as long as possible. Death fed off this torment. The long, drawn-out process of scourging, beating, and the cross allowed Death to dance with its victim.

None had ever taken the punishment that this Son had received. Yet, every time Death moved in to suffocate Him, it was harshly repelled. The life force of the Son was unlike anything it had ever come across. So it crouched, obsessively watching its prey and waiting to pounce and devour.

For three hours, the Son had moved His bloodied back on the post of the cross. A victim of crucifixion was placed so that he was forced to move his torso up and down to keep air in his lungs. If he stopped, his lungs would fill, causing the victim to drown in his own blood.

The Romans placed a small seat under the sufferer, giving a sense of resting. But as the victim tried to sit he would slip off, sending shock waves of pain throughout the pierced nerves. Death smiled at the genius of this brutality.

A moment after the Son sipped of the wine-vinegar, He spoke. "Tetelestai!"

Death cocked its head. This strange, single word meant "it is finished" or "paid in full." Maybe this Son was finally going to die, for He spoke nonsense.

The Son bowed His head.

"Now!" growled Death. As it came to clutch His neck, it was once again thrown below the cross. Consternation filled Death, pinned to the earth and unable to look away from the Son's eyes.

Staring down at Death, the Son spoke His last words, "Father, into Your hands I commit My spirit." Death, now loosened from invisible restraints, lurched forward! But the instant it touched the Son's heart, it was again thrown below the cross. Quietly, the Son's spirit departed without the icy touch of Death.

How could Death not destroy the Son on its terms? It was as if the Son had decided His moment of departure. A raging roar of loss was loosed from Death and the earth shook with its fury. "Where is my victory? Where is my sting?"

Lord Jesus Christ, have mercy upon me.

Lord, to know that even death could not hold You
causes my heart to swell with faith.
I ask You to make me as an ambassador of life.
I want to reach the physically dying
and those who are wasting away spiritually.
I want abundant living waters to flow from me,
and I desire true life to be a byproduct of my obedience.
In a world dark with death,
let Your light illuminate the darkness through my life.

Lord Jesus Christ, have mercy upon me.

The curtain
will separate the
Holy Place
from the
Most Holy Place.

Exodus 26:33

Torn

Eternal Spirit of the chainless Mind!
Brightest in dungeons, Liberty! thou art,
For there thy habitation is the heart—
The heart which love of Thee alone can bind.
Lord Byron, "On the Castle of Chillon"

Make a curtain of blue, purple and scarlet yarn and finely twisted linen, with cherubim worked into it by a skilled craftsman. Hang it with gold hooks on four posts of acacia wood overlaid with gold and standing on four silver bases. Hang the curtain from the clasps and place the ark of the Testimony behind the curtain.
Exodus 26:31–33

And when Jesus had cried out again in a loud voice, he gave up his spirit. At that moment the curtain of the temple was torn in two from top to bottom. The earth shook and the rocks split. The tombs broke open and the bodies of many holy people who had died were raised to life. They came out of the tombs, and after Jesus' resurrection they went into the holy city and appeared to many people.
Matthew 27:50–53

The young priest-in-training was quite concerned over the events that had been rapidly unfolding around him. The only facts he knew for sure were that there was a strange meeting of the Jewish council this morning that led to the crucifixion of the false prophet from Galilee, and that the rest of the day was dedicated to celebrating the Passover. After a morning of deliberations, most of the chief priests returned to the temple to fulfill their duties, but many were strangely quiet and some seemed to be brooding.

About noon, as the Jewish men were bringing their sacrifices to the temple, a dark cloud mass, covering as far as the eye could see, rolled over Jerusalem and blocked out the sun with a curtain of darkness. Quickly, torches and lanterns were lit. The air was thick with tension, and some wondered aloud if Messiah was about to return for His chosen people. For three hours, the sacrifices continued.

At the time High Priest Caiaphas entered into the Holy Place to make supplication before the veil, an echoed cry that sounded like the voice of God traveled the length of the holy city. Grabbing a nearby pillar, the young priest braced himself. He felt as if he was about to be sick.

Then the earthquake hit. It was strong enough to make the young man wonder if the temple was going to fall and crush him.

Suddenly, several chief priests came running from the inner portion of the sanctuary. Their priestly garments were torn, and some even cried, "Ichabod," as they fled in terror.

Stopping an elderly priest, the young man asked, "What has happened?"

The frightened man looked as if he had seen the walking dead. "It is torn! It is torn! The high priest was making supplication before the veil and it tore from the ceiling to the floor. Why has the Lord's spirit departed us?" It was too much for the terrified old man. He started to weep, then continued to run with an invisible dread.

The young priest slumped to the floor against the pillar, holding his head in his hands. How could this be? For the first time since the Israelites' return from captivity, the sacrifices would not be completed on the Passover. The veil was torn, allowing anyone to view into the Most Holy Place.

Why had God allowed this abomination? Or had the Lord caused this? The young man succumbed to the tears that had been building. Grabbing his garment, he violently tore it from top to bottom.

Lord Jesus Christ, have mercy upon me.

We have this hope as an anchor for our soul,
that Jesus Christ, our High Priest,
entered the inner sanctuary behind the curtain,
on our behalf and He has become our High Priest forever.
He entered the Most Holy Place once and for all,
by His own blood, and obtained eternal redemption.
Now we may serve the Living God
with unblemished consciences.
Let us approach the throne of grace with boldness,
so that we may receive mercy
and find grace to help us in our time of need.
Therefore, since we have confidence to
enter the Most Holy Place by the blood of Jesus,
by a new and living way opened for us
through the veil, that is His body,
let us draw near to God with sincere hearts
and full assurance of faith.

Lord Jesus Christ, have mercy upon me.

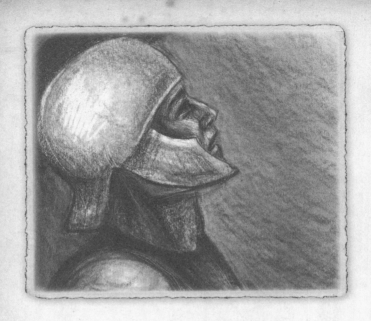

Surely this was a
righteous man
[and] the
Son of God!

Luke 23:47 and Mark 15:39

Centurion

I shall light a candle of understanding in thine heart, which shall not be put out.

Apocrypha, 2 Esdras 14:25

I, the LORD have called you in righteousness; I will take hold of your hand. I will keep you and will make you to be a covenant for the people and a light for the Gentiles, to open eyes that are blind, to free captives from prison and to release from the dungeon those who sit in darkness.

Isaiah 42:6–7

When the centurion (who stood there in front of Jesus) and those with him who were guarding Jesus heard his cry (saw the earthquake) and saw how he died, they were terrified. (The centurion) praised God and said, "Surely this was a righteous man [and] the Son of God!" When all the people who had gathered to witness this sight saw what took place, they beat their breasts and went away. But all those who knew him, including the women who had followed him from Galilee, stood at a distance, watching these things.

Matthew 27:54; Mark 15:39; and Luke 23:47–49

As I have already explained to you, Flavius, my tale of the execution of Jesus of Nazareth has been a great mystery to me. But now I tell you the oddest part of my story.

As leader of the execution squad, I had been close enough to hear all of the Nazarene's words from the cross. Seven times He spoke, and each discourse seemed to undo my heart a bit more. I can only explain this with a crude illustration. It was like removing the gear, piece by piece, from my faithful steed's back. When he is finally free of his tackle, he can run unhindered. Slowly, this supposed criminal's words were causing me to remove obstacles of doubt in my mind. When He cried His final words, "It is finished!" my men and I fell to the earth terrified.

Flavius, you must understand that He did not die from crucifixion. He chose to die as if He dominated death itself. The skies darkened in mourning. The earth shook in fury. Every element of creation seemed to grieve His departure. Even those that had surrounded Him to find amusement in His suffering started to pound their chests in the Jewish custom of grieving. Quickly, they crept away, wearing cloaks of shame and misery. A small group of His followers stood back and wept, waiting for the chance to remove and bury His decimated body.

In all my years leading this century of men and overseeing countless crucifixions, I have never observed signs like this. I stood to my feet and looked at the Man on the cross. Even in death, He possessed an air of absolute peace. All I could do was declare, "Surely this was a righteous man and the Son of God!"

So, Flavius, as I have already revealed, I must end my commission as a centurion in the Roman army. Part of this falls on your shoulders, my friend. For it was the tale of how this Holy Man first visited your home in Capernaum that opened my heart to the possibility of His claim. Hearing about and seeing your dear child healed continues to be a point of conversation among the officers. Imagine, a Roman centurion inviting a Rabbi to heal his child. You are practically a Hebrew yourself. I still laugh at the words He spoke about you, "Surely I have not seen such a great faith in all of Israel."

Now, Flavius, my tale ends. I shall be departing in a fortnight back to Troas to become a simple farmer and to spread the story of the crucified Son of God. May our paths cross once again in the afterlife.

Lord Jesus Christ, have mercy upon me.

You declared that those who witnessed and
believed were blessed.
Yet, You also said that those who have not seen and
believed are greatly blessed.
I believe in You, Lord Christ.
May I pass Your blessing onto others every day.

Lord Jesus Christ, have mercy upon me.

He protects **all**
his bones,
not one of them
will be broken.

Psalm 34:20

Many of you, as I recall . . . complain of this . . . dryness of soul, this heaviness and dullness of mind, devoid of the power to penetrate the profound and hidden truths of God, devoid too, entirely or for the most part, of the sweetness of Spirit. What is that my brothers, but a longing to be kissed.

St. Bernard of Clairvaux

And I will pour out on the house of David and the inhabitants of Jerusalem a spirit of grace and supplication. They will look on me, the one they have pierced, and they will mourn for him as one mourns for an only child, and grieve bitterly for him as one grieves for a firstborn son.

Zechariah 12:10

Now it was the day of Preparation, and the next day was to be a special Sabbath. Because the Jews did not want the bodies left on the crosses during the Sabbath, they asked Pilate to have the legs broken and the bodies taken down. The soldiers therefore came and broke the legs of the first man who had been crucified with Jesus, and then those of the other. But when they came to Jesus and found that he was already dead, they did not break his legs. Instead, one of the soldiers pierced Jesus' side with a spear, bringing a sudden flow of blood and water. The man who saw it has given testimony, and his testimony is true. He knows that he tells the truth, and he testifies so that you also may believe. These things happened so that the scripture would be fulfilled: "Not one of his bones will be broken," and, as another scripture says, "They will look on the one they have pierced."

John 19: 31–37

The Creator, after designating First Man "Adam," had asked him to name all the other creatures of the earth. With childlike glee, Adam named them, one by one. As the game of designation progressed, he realized no counterpart for him could be found. Where was the "she" to compliment his "he-ness"?

On the day that he felt his heart would finally burst with loneliness, his Father walked into the garden. They discussed his aloneness in great detail.

Even as he fell into a divine deep slumber, he knew his Father would mend his incomplete heart. The tender, celestial hand of an Omnipotent God entered into Adam's side. What Adam did not realize was that there was a gift the Creator had hidden very close to his heart. Reaching for this hidden treasure, the Creator of all seen and unseen removed the masterpiece of creation that was hidden in His child.

After Adam awoke, this secret legacy would be revealed. The Creator would present to Adam a bride that would bring him completeness and overwhelming joy.

The day was rapidly coming to a close, and the soldiers knew the victims must soon be removed and buried according to Jewish law. They had a special process of final elimination they called the crurifragium. Going to the first thief on the right of Jesus, they smashed his legs. The prisoner screamed in agony, but quickly expired of shock. The guard noticed that this one seemed to smile in peace during the last few seconds of his life. The thief on the left shrieked as they crushed his legs. He thrashed so violently that his life ended with a gurgling scream.

Already recognizing His departure, and not wanting to inflict any more damage on the body of Jesus, the soldiers opted for another form of proof to testify of His death. One of the guards grabbed a spear and thrust it under Jesus' ribs, straight into His heart. As blood and water flowed, an invisible gift also emerged. For in this Man's heart, there was a hidden secret. A bride, that would bring Him completeness and overwhelming joy, would very soon be revealed.

Lord Jesus Christ, have mercy upon me.

I come and fall at your feet in awe.
For what other way am I to respond to Your call:
"Come forth, my bride."?
Your blood covers my sins,
and Your water of life engulfs my spirit.
You have cleansed me,
and You have prepared me to be a spotless bride.
So now I await the great anticipation,
the wedding feast of the Lamb,
and I imagine beyond imagination what that day will bring.

Lord Jesus Christ, have mercy upon me.

Therefore my **heart** is glad
and my tongue rejoices;
my **body** will also rest secure,
because you will **not**
abandon me to the **grave**,
nor will you let your **Holy** One
see decay.

Psalm 16:9-10

Taken

Nor deem the irrevocable Past,
As wholly wasted, wholly vain,
If, rising on its wrecks, at last
To something nobler we attain.
Henry Wadsworth Longfellow, "The Ladder of St. Augustine"

Some women were watching from a distance. Among them were Mary Magdalene, Mary the mother of James the younger and of Joses [the mother of Zebedee's sons], and Salome. In Galilee these women had followed him and cared for his needs. Many other women who had come up with him to Jerusalem were also there. It was Preparation Day (that is, the day before the Sabbath). So as evening approached, Joseph of Arimathea, a prominent member of the Council [a rich, upright man who had himself become a secret disciple of Jesus because he feared the Jews and], who was himself waiting for the kingdom of God, went boldly to Pilate and asked for Jesus' body. He was accompanied by Nicodemus, the man who earlier had visited Jesus by night. Pilate was surprised to hear that he was already dead. Summoning the centurion, he asked him if Jesus had already died. When he learned from the centurion that it was so, he gave the body to Joseph. Nicodemus brought a mixture of myrrh and aloes, about seventy-five pounds. Taking Jesus' body, the two of them wrapped it, with the spices, in strips of linen. This was in accordance with Jewish burial customs.

Mark 15:40–45 and John 19:39–40

"It may be a foolish move, my friend, but it is necessary," Joseph spoke in hushed tones. In full agreement, Nicodemus replied, "If only we had been as fearless while He lived. But I will not cower again." The two men were rapidly approaching Pilate's presence.

They had both argued for Jesus' release, but received only the jeers and antagonism of the council. Heartbroken, they watched His trial, torture, and death, all from afar. Shoulder to shoulder, they wept as they saw His head slump in a final breath. At the moment of His expiration, something awoke in both men. The respect and place of honor they had both possessed were now bile in their throats.

Joseph of Arimathea was a wealthy and reputable member of the Sanhedrin. The first day he heard Jesus in the temple, he was convinced that the long-awaited Christ had arrived. But the fear of losing his position of authority kept his love for the Rabbi shrouded in secrecy. Nicodemus was one of the most educated and respected teachers in Israel. His study of the Scriptures had convinced him that Jesus of Nazareth was Messiah, and he quietly awaited the day of His disclosure.

When Jesus entered Jerusalem a week ago, they were both prepared to bow their knees upon the revelation of His sovereignty. But circumstances had taken a tragic turn.

They now determined together that the death of their friend would not be the departure of their faith. Boldly, they asked Pilate for the body of Jesus. "An odd request," thought Pilate. These men were not family. They were not afraid of entering Pilate's home, nor of defilement upon handling a dead body. It was a daring if not foolhardy request. To honor their audacity, he would grant their boon.

Hurrying back to Golgotha, they spoke a few words of comfort to the grieving women that stood at the foot of the tree. Another man, the young disciple of Jesus, helped lower the body from the cross. With rapid and willful purpose, they washed the gashed corpse and wrapped it in a layer of cloth. After applying the aromatic spices, the body was wrapped again. Though their prior actions were born of cowardice, their present open confession left no doubt about how they would now and forever view the Prophet from Galilee.

Lord Jesus Christ, have mercy upon me.

I can think of too many times
when I have kept You hidden
from those that needed a word of Your love.
Forgive me for my times of cowardice,
and fill me with Your Spirit.
Let true boldness be an integral part of my character.
Open wide the gates of opportunity to share Your truth,
and help me to embrace those You love.

Lord Jesus Christ, have mercy upon me.

He was assigned a **grave**
with the wicked, and
with the **rich** in his death,
though he had done **no** violence,
nor was **any deceit**
in his mouth.

Isaiah 53:9

O world invisible, we view thee,
O world intangible, we touch thee,
O world unknowable, we know thee,
Inapprehensible, we clutch thee!
Francis Thompson, "In No Strange Land"

At the place where Jesus was crucified, there was a garden, and in the garden a new tomb, in which no one had ever been laid. Joseph took the body [and] wrapped it in a clean linen cloth. Because it was the Jewish day of Preparation and since the tomb was nearby, they laid Jesus there. He rolled a big stone in front of the entrance to the tomb and went away. Mary Magdalene and the other Mary were sitting there opposite of the tomb. The women who had come with Jesus from Galilee followed Joseph and saw the tomb and how his body was laid in it. Then they went home and prepared spices and perfumes. But they rested on the Sabbath in obedience to the commandment.
John 19:41–42; Matthew 27:59–61; and Luke 23:55–56

In the rush to entomb the body before sunset, the women and men set their grieving aside until the task was complete. They prepared the body to the best of their abilities, and carefully placed Him on the cold stone shelf in the fresh-hewn tomb. Mary Magdalene, standing on the outside of the garden grave, thought it odd that such a dismal place should be so beautiful. The setting sun, finally breaking through the day's dark clouds, shone off the semi-polished rock that had not had time to gather dust or feel the effects of age. The men carefully released a flat circular stone from an elevated track in the front of the tomb. The rounded stone boomed as it locked into place. Firmly planted, it would take a large group of men to roll the several-hundred-pound rock away.

The crash of the stone caused the small gathering to shudder. The reality of their loss descended upon them in a sudden deluge. Their beloved Master was dead. Mary Magdalene fell to the ground as if to faint. Quietly, almost imperceptibly, she wept. As her tears became a tempest, she remembered the day they met.

As a woman filled with self-rage and insane lust, her existence had been filled with the pain and distress of an unsavory lifestyle. Her hometown of Magdala, on the coast of the Galilean Sea and known for its prostitution rings, was a cancer to her soul. She had been a woman with no control of her mind or body. Mary was entombed inside her head, having the ability to see out, but with no control of her actions. This would often manifest itself in multiple personalities that arrived and departed as they saw fit. That was until He arrived.

When she first noticed Jesus, all she wanted to do was throw herself into the sea and end her misery. He was so lovely, so holy, and this caused her to feel the weight of her sin and shame.

He spoke a simple word that brought her to her right mind. In an instant, she was free. He had seen the invisible demons inside her and addressed them with unmitigated authority. The insubstantial woman of torment became the tangible Mary.

From that moment, she followed Him. Mary Magdalene would serve Him as long as she was able.

Sitting in front of His grave, she wiped her eyes and prepared to leave. Mary determined to tend His grave for the rest of her life, so that none would forget God's Son.

Lord Jesus Christ, have mercy upon me.

There have been times in my life, Lord,
where the loss of control has ensnared me
with dread, fear, and tormenting anxiety.
My inability to dictate the circumstances
that have affected my life,
such as health, finances, or the decisions of others,
has created in me a madness
that hides in my head like a stinger.

But You always remind me that if I trust in You
and do not lean on my understanding,
You will direct and steady my steps.
Help me to put the direction of my life into Your hands
and to not foolishly grasp for it myself.
Set me free from the tomb of my mind
and draw me into the freedom of Your guidance and peace.

Lord Jesus Christ, have mercy upon me.

O God, you are my God,
earnestly I seek you;
my soul thirsts for you,
my body longs for you,
in a dry and weary land
where there is no water.

Psalm 63:1

> *What is essential is invisible to the eye.*
> **Antoine de Saint-Exupéry, *The Little Prince***

The next day, the one after Preparation Day, the chief priests and the Pharisees went to Pilate. "Sir," they said, "we remember that while he was still alive that deceiver said, 'After three days I will rise again.' So give the order for the tomb to be made secure until the third day. Otherwise, his disciples may come and steal the body and tell the people that he has been raised from the dead. This last deception will be worse than the first." "Take a guard," Pilate answered. "Go, make the tomb as secure as you know how." So they went and made the tomb secure by putting a seal on the stone and posting the guard.
> **Matthew 27:62–66**

"Lucis, the charge I now give you is the most important of our creation." Gabriel spoke with urgency, but he also seemed ready to explode with joyous anticipation. "You are to be present at the Unveiling and record all that you witness. This chronicle of the Mystery Revealed will be passed down for eternity. Before you depart for the garden, I would like to open your eyes to a variety of dramatis personae who have been part of this story."

Lucis was as apprehensive as a heavenly being could be. He knew this was the moment for which he was created, and all creatures from time without end would hear his account.

Instantly, Lucis found himself in a sullied back alley in Jerusalem. A man huddled against the wall, shaking. Rocking back and forth, he mumbled the same phrase again and again. "It should have been my cross. It should have been mine . . ."

Fading away, Lucis found himself in the bedchambers of the high priest. Caiaphas was in a fitful sleep when he suddenly awoke, sat straight up in his bed, and let loose a terrified scream, "Crucify him!"

In a moment, Lucis stood in the writing room of the prefect of the Judean Province. Pilate was agonizing over a letter he was composing for Rome. Of course, he did not intend to send the dispatch unless asked, but a good defense was better if it was well prepared. Slamming his fist to the writing table, he cried, "Damned be that manipulative council and the trouble they've caused me!"

Whisked away again, Lucis found himself in the home of a centurion. Endless tears flowed from the centurion's face as he composed a letter.

Lucis traveled to several sites over the next few hours. He saw this narrative from a multitude of perspectives. His next-to-last stop was a darkened, small upper room, where the disciples who had abandoned Him hid. Their only covering seemed to be an all-enveloping depression. Even with angelic understanding, he was stunned at the vast amount of emotions the Son's death evoked in these tender humans.

While still caught in his thoughts, Lucis found himself in front of the garden tomb. The sun was cresting the horizon while a few sleepy guards stood at half-hearted attention. As the earth slowly began to tremble, Lucis pulled out his parchment and pen. "Ready yourself, Lucis, for the world is about to erupt . . ."

Lord Jesus Christ, have mercy upon me.

I wait for You, Jesus.

Lord Jesus Christ, have mercy upon me.

Death has been
swallowed up
in victory
Where, O death,
is your victory?
Where, O death,
is your sting?

1 Corinthians 15:54-55

The Unveiling

If you shut up truth and bury it under the ground, it will but grow, and gather to itself such explosive power that the day it bursts through it will blow up everything in its way.

Émile Zola

After the Sabbath, very early on the first day of the week, just after sunrise, Mary Magdalene, Salome, and the other Mary went to look at the tomb and anoint Jesus' body. They asked themselves, "Who will roll the stone away from the entrance of the tomb?" There was a violent earthquake, for an angel of the Lord came down from heaven, and going to the tomb, rolled back the stone and sat on it. His appearance was like lightning, and his clothes were white as snow. The guards were so afraid of him that they shook and became like dead men. Mary Magdalene came running to Simon Peter and the other disciple, the one Jesus loved, and said, "They have taken the Lord out of the tomb, and we do not know where they have put him!"

The angel said to the women, "Why are you looking for the living among the dead? Do not be afraid, for I know that you are looking for Jesus, who was crucified. He is not here; He has risen like He said. Come and see the place where he lay. Then go quickly and tell the disciples: 'He has risen from the dead and is going ahead of you into Galilee. There you will see him.'"

Matthew 28:1–7; Mark 16:1–7; and John 20:1–2
(author's paraphrase)

Lucis stood near the tomb, watching and recording the most important events of history as they unfolded around him. The heavenly host had gathered en masse to witness the Unveiling. Suddenly, with an explosion exceeding that of creation, the detonation of resurrection poured forth from the tiny tomb in an ever-widening sphere. First, it hit the surrounding garden, causing a shudder throughout the entire planet. The sudden flash revealed an angel of awesome proportions to the terrified guards. Reverential fear rendered them instantly unconscious. Even as they fell to the earth, the angel rolled back the stone from the tomb and sat upon it with a childlike glee.

As the sphere of resurrection continued to expand, it plowed through the earth, reaching the depths of Sheol. Dark angels and their evil lord crumpled into the small mounds in an attempt to avoid destruction. The roar of life that tore through them masked their screams. As the explosion increased, it picked up greater momentum. Before the flinch of a seraphim's wing, it had consumed the solar system and the entire angelic host. In veneration, they fell prostrate before the blast. Farther and farther it grew, until it overtook all of eternity. In a move that only the Godhead could carry out, the explosion broke through the fabric of eternity into the All in All.

In an omnipotent backdraft, resurrection unexpectedly turned inward, contracting back toward the source of the discharge. As the ball of life now imploded, it sent a second wave inward until it reached the Incarnation. Resurrection would be contained in One Being.

All became still, except for one hidden being that seemed unscathed by the explosion. Death, initially taking cover, now cautiously appeared as a triumphant victor. But before it could open its mouth, it froze in terror. In the tomb, it observed the astonishing countenance of He-Who-Was-Now-Alive.

Death became immobilized as its Antithesis approached. Touching Death's brow, the Son spoke, "You are forever castrated of your power. From this point forward, you will decrease and I will increase. Your reign is done."

But Lucis was far from finished. A new age was beginning that would make the first age seem a simple foreword to the history of eternity. Lucis smiled, knowing the next few weeks should prove quite interesting. In that moment, he wrote the first words that came to his spirit. "Alive. He is alive. The mystery is revealed."

Lord Jesus Christ, have mercy upon me.

Death has been swallowed up in victory
Where, O death, is your victory?
Where, O death, is your sting?

Lord Jesus Christ, have mercy upon me.

Acknowledgments

I gratefully recognize those who have been necessary to the completion of this work.

My beloved, Cheryl. You are not only my best friend, but also the one who has thoroughly convinced me to walk confidently in my call. Imagine, after twenty years of marriage, joy still increases daily. Thank you for making me laugh, cry, and laugh so hard that I cry.

My four children: Antonio, for your friendship; Coeli, for your transparent heart; Kayla, for your love for life; and Hunter, for our wrestle-time. We have many new adventures ahead!

My amazing mom, Bonnie West. Thanks for teaching me to dream. I love our scrabble games.

My parents, Larry and Mariette Small, who showed me faith when I was faithless.

My siblings: Shane, Audra, Jared, Jordan, and Lisa. You are often in my thoughts. Christopher, I miss you so much.

My editor, Lori Janke, for your thorough grammatical skills, but more for your insightful comments, constant encouragement, and delightful sense of humor.

My discerning narrative, historical, and theological editors: Dr. Walter Fletcher and Molly Wren. Wow! Can I keep you guys?

All the amazing team at Providence House Publishers who brought the vision to pass, but especially my managing editor, Nancy Wise, who treated this work as an act of worship; my production manager, Holly Jones, who kept the wheels from falling off; and my designer, LeAnna Massingille, who somehow read my heart and transposed it to print.

My board: Joe Morrone, Ken Janke, Tom Nichols, and Michael Fleming. You always "got" my back!

Wonder Voyage staff: I sometimes speculate whether our events are just an excuse to bring us together. You are godsends as staff, but also dear friends and comrades in arms.

Our distinguished artist, Jenny Slaver. Your lovingly worked art will draw multitudes onto the via crucis. Thank you for your passion, vision, and time.

Father Sean Lawlor and the Esker Retreat Center in Athenry County, Galway, Ireland. Dominick's Hill and the stations on the grounds of Esker have transported me to places I never imagined.

Appendix A
A Community Worship Experience

The via crucis was initially birthed as a community worship experience. I was speaking at a three-day event at a Christian school on the theme of the cross. Every day, we covered five stations, ending with a time of repentance before a cross that had been erected in the auditorium. The powerful reaction of the students convinced me of the validity of the via crucis on a large scale.

The following information is designed to help direct you in leading a larger group of participants in the via crucis. Those of a Catholic or Anglican background will be more aware of the intricacies of a via crucis service, but any worshiping community will benefit.

Time

A via crucis experience can be completed within two hours or it can be modified to be completed during a weekend retreat. The most important aspects to consider for timing are:

- How many stations will you cover and how long will you spend per station?
- Will you incorporate song into the worship experience?
- Will you go over scriptures, readings, prayers, or a selection?
- How many people will be involved in the via crucis?
- Will you allow moments of meditation throughout the experience?

All of these questions factor into the amount of time you will want to devote to a via crucis experience.

Selection

The importance of the selection process has mainly to do with the journey of the via crucis. You must be willing to take the participants from the beginning of the passion to the burial of Jesus. Depending upon the time allowed, you will want to make a careful selection of the stations you choose. You may want to go with the traditional fourteen stations, the biblical fourteen stations (see appendix B), or choose a variety. In this book, we include forty stations you may want to consider. The number and choice of stations can vary greatly, depending upon what you want the worshippers to focus. The focus could be the cost of the cross, the sacrifice of Christ, or how people reacted to His sacrifice. The choice is yours. We recommend, however, that unless it is a Good Friday service, you take the group to the resurrection station titled "The Unveiling."

Those Involved

We have found that the more individuals involved in the via crucis, the more the group benefits. As you divide into stations, consider combining two to three people for each devotional. If you have three participants, one can read the Scriptures, one can present the reading, and one can offer prayers.

Do not feel bound to the specific reading provided. Allowing the participants to take some time to pray and to speak out the inspiration of their hearts about the Scriptures is awe inspiring.

Art

Creating art around the stations is a wonderful worship experience. This obviously works better during a retreat setting where more time is allotted. We have done everything from having artists paint renditions of the stations during a two-hour period to students creating an artistic interpretation of individual stations out of natural materials. The sky's the limit for artistic expression.

Another unique artistic expression is with dramatic readings, or the addition of a theatrical interpretation. Most of the readings for the via crucis can be easily translated as a first-person character. If you have a particularly gifted group of actors, they may be able to give their artistic interpretation of the readings. Some examples would be the centurion writing to his friend about his experience, Malchus at the arrest, or Veronica as she wipes Jesus' face.

Think about having a cross centered during the event. The cross can be simple and crudely constructed, or hung on the wall and highlighted by light.

Communion

The most effective way to bring a via crucis experience to a close is with a time of Eucharist or Communion. The via crucis, by its very nature, draws pilgrims toward the heart of Christ. At the point of resurrection, many participants will be ready to solidify decisions that they have made during the course of the event. There is no greater impact on those choices than participation in the Lord's Supper. This will usually take some forethought, so plan carefully.

Appendix B
The Traditional Stations

The traditional stations of the cross sanctioned by the Catholic Church are as follows (page numbers corresponding to this book follow each station title).

In 1991 and 1994, Pope John Paul II celebrated the scriptural stations of the cross in the Coliseum at Rome. They were as follows:

Many stations end, appropriately, with a fifteenth station: The Unveiling.

About the Artist

Jenny Slaver has been drawing since she could hold a crayon. She met Shawn Small at a camping retreat he hosted while she was still in high school. One night, around the campfire, Shawn affirmed her gift for creativity and art. Jenny claims that night as one of the first moments that she truly began to acknowledge herself as an artist. Since then, Shawn has been a diehard advocate for Jenny's art.

While creating all forty original pieces for *The Via Crucis*, Jenny was a student at the Memphis College of Art. Her own words best describe why she took on such a monumental project at such a busy time in her life: "The cross is the sweetest intermingling of tragedy and beauty. It is the very reason for art. Without Christ's sacrifice there would be no beauty in the world; no overflow of joy, no hope for the human heart. For me, without the cross there is no art."

Jenny acknowledges the art of Kathe Kollowitz, whose work greatly influenced her while she worked on *The Via Crucis*. She is thrilled to begin her career by drawing the cornerstone of her artistic inspiration, and hopes to use art as a therapeutic healing tool for those who have experienced traumatic pain and loss.

About the Author

For ten years, Shawn Small was a youth minister in the Dallas metro area. In 1999, he took a year-long sabbatical to find God's heart for his future. The result of that time was the launching of Wonder Voyage Missions in the year 2000.

Wonder Voyage is a unique organization dedicated to educating and leading groups into the ancient Christian practice of pilgrimage and in life-transforming service trips around the world.

Shawn has had the privilege of leading hundreds of people to locations around the world that include Wales, Jamaica, Greece, Guatemala, and Peru.

Although he leads several retreats a year, Shawn considers himself first and foremost a storyteller. This is his first endeavor at publishing in his unique storytelling style. He and his wife, Cheryl, reside in Flower Mound, Texas. They have four children.

Wonder Voyage Missions

Wonder Voyage Missions can be expressed in one exceptional idea: Journey. A non-profit organization, Wonder Voyage Missions is dedicated to providing the modern day sojourner with the unique opportunity of pursuing the heart of God in extraordinary locations, through unparalleled opportunities.

Wonder Voyage focuses on six primary principles:

- **Community Venture**
  Wonder Voyage desires to take communities that follow Christ and draw them nearer to the heart of God and to the hearts of each other. We are an ecumenical organization committed to the Word of God, the unity of the saints, and a living, passionate Savior.

- **Voyage of Exploration**
  At Wonder Voyage, we avoid the tourist traps and seize life. From exotic locations to remarkable experiences, Wonder Voyage takes you to the hidden scenes of life. On a Wonder Voyage, exploration and adventure are inevitable. The via crucis is just one path that we offer pilgrims along the way.

- **Customizing the Event**
  At Wonder Voyage, we recognize that every group has a unique personality. We assess your group's desires and objectives to fashion an event that will become an exceptional and personal experience for your group.

- **Encounter Moments**
  Every event consists of defining reflections that we refer to as Encounter Moments. God often orchestrates encounters for your team through exploration, storytelling, journaling, or team reflection.

- **Handling the Details**

  Wonder Voyage allows you to enjoy your event instead of juggling the vital details such as transportation, food, lodging, and coordination that often keep a team leader buried in minutia. Our experienced staff does the work and you enjoy the benefits.

- **Global Possibilities**

  Wonder Voyage is established in several locations around the world, but we are willing to go anywhere a team desires. What about a domestic pilgrimage to historic New Orleans or the sprawling streets of New York City? Or maybe you have a heart for the rolling hills of Ireland or the jungles of Costa Rica? Wonder Voyage has global possibilities.

For more information on Wonder Voyage trips or to host a via crucis retreat, please contact

PO Box 2135
Coppell, TX 75019
Office: 972-355-1712

www.wondervoyage.com
www.theviacrucis.com